OVERCOMING OBSTACLES with S P U N K !

The Keys to Leadership & Goal-Setting

Titles by L. Diane Wolfe
Published by Dancing Lemur Press, L.L.C.

THE CIRCLE OF FRIENDS BOOKS
Book I ... Lori
Book II ... Sarah
Book III ... James
Book IV ... Mike
Book V ... Heather

Overcoming Obstacles with SPUNK!
The Keys to Leadership & Goal-Setting

OVERCOMING OBSTACLES
with SPUNK!

The Keys to Leadership & Goal-Setting

L. Diane Wolfe

DANCING LEMUR PRESS, L.L.C.
Fremont, North Carolina
www.dancinglemurpress.com

Published by Dancing Lemur Press, L.L.C.
P.O. Box 383, Pikeville, North Carolina, 27863-0383
www.dancinglemurpress.com

ISBN: 978-0-9816210-2-9 / 0-9816210-2-3

Printed in the United States of America

Cover design by C.R.W.
Back cover photo by Vance Allen

Publisher's Cataloging-in-Publication data

Wolfe, L. Diane.
    Overcoming obstacles with SPUNK! : the keys to leadership & goal-setting / L. Diane Wolfe.
    p. cm.
    ISBN 978-0-9816210-2-9
1. Self-help techniques. 2. Self-actualization (Psychology). 3. Life skills —Handbooks, manuals, etc. 4. Success —Psychological aspects. 5. Self-esteem. I. Overcoming obstacles with SPUNK! : the keys to leadership and goal setting. II. Title.

HQ2037 .W655 2009
646.7/20—dc22
2008909597

Dedicated to those who dare to dream,
strive to achieve, and refuse to surrender!

Special thanks to all whom contributed to this book.
We cannot overcome and succeed alone, and I
consider your assistance and support a blessing!

And to the late Larry Etheridge,
who was an incredible example of leadership
and success for all who knew him!

Contents

Introduction

Remember when you were a child? The world held so many possibilities! The future lay before you like a wide-open road, ready to be explored. You could go anywhere you wanted, pursue any profession, and achieve any dream. There were no inhibitions or rules. Your dreams and ambitions glowed bright with potential. And like the night before Christmas, you were bursting with eager anticipation!

Somewhere along the way, a negative reality began to take control. The dreams of youth faded, replaced by adult expectations and safe choices. Passion turned into pessimism and worry replaced desire. The joy of living slowly lost foothold to the struggle to survive. Your once bright future slowly vanished, obscured by the dark clouds of doubt.

If the words "stuck in a rut" describe your life, you are not alone! Mediocrity describes the lives of many people today. Settling for a life that is less than fulfilling, they fail to pursue their dreams or realize their full potential. Their lives lack purpose and drive. I know, because I was once one of those people!

Eventually, this feisty redhead decided she'd had enough and began seeking a better life. When I first began studying the components of success, I noticed several reoccurring themes. Despite the variations and numerous formulas, certain elements appeared universal. I eventually realized there were five distinct Keys.

These five Keys- developing a positive attitude, developing people skills, raising self-esteem, overcoming fear, and setting goals- form the foundation of success. They unlock the door to overcoming obstacles and developing leadership. When all five Keys are applied together, they unlock one's full potential.

"Overcoming Obstacles with SPUNK!" originally began as a goal-setting seminar and eventually spawned a leadership seminar as well. With the help of seven other authors and speakers- David Ambrose, p.m. terrell, Darlene Wofford, Jocelyn Andersen, Bob Johnson, C. Denise Sutton, and Bill Wilson- those seminars transformed into this very book. Each author brought an insightful new twist to the five Keys, and I am forever grateful for their contributions. None of us reaches success alone!

Ready to revisit those dreams and aspirations of youth? No inhibitions, no restrictions, just possibilities. All it takes is five Keys- and little bit of SPUNK!

L. Diane Wolfe
a.k.a. "Spunk On A Stick"

1

Overcoming Obstacles
and Achieving Goals

Life is all about overcoming.

Living to the fullest requires determination. We must possess purpose and drive. We need set goals and a positive attitude. Fear must be conquered. Leadership traits and people skills are vital. To live a life filled with enrichment and satisfaction, we need some spunk!

What is the secret? We have seen others experience great personal triumphs and satisfaction. How does one achieve this level of fulfillment? Surely there must be a pill or potion we can consume that will transform our lives into something more! Unfortunately, life doesn't work in this manner. True success requires effort, and only we can make it happen.

All of God's creatures were designed to live for a purpose. Achievement is part of our very makeup. Sadly, many of us get so caught up in the struggle just to survive that the result is an existence rather than a life. We lose sight of our purpose. This is not how we were intended to live, though. We need to rekindle the purpose within and ignite our spirits once again.

Will change be required? Of course! We can't continue on our current path. If we expect life to improve, we cannot remain mired in the same patterns. Those habits created our current situation and must be abandoned if we desire different results. It's irrational to keep using a blue pen and hope it will one day transform into a red pen!

Change will be required in areas outside of the physical as well. It's not just those daily patterns, but also the habits of our mind that prevent us from achieving more in life. Our attitude is a powerful influence on our world and the deciding factor in our ultimate success. The ability to deal with other people is an important skill. Fear also begins in the mind. All of these mental traits and behaviors contribute to our overall success and fulfillment as human beings.

Too often, we allow circumstances to dictate our lives. We feel we lack in education or do not possess the right skills to succeed. We point to our upbringing and what we did not possess or experience as a child. Sometimes we even blame others for the conditions under which we now reside. Regardless of the circumstances, though, there is no good excuse for failure. We are the ones in control of our destiny.

Victory is not about waiting for circumstances- it's creating our own. Wallowing in mud will only make us dirty, and wallowing in problems only makes us helpless. We must assume responsibility and create our own opportunities. Our placement in life can only be attributed to one living person, and the sooner we realize this truth, the sooner we can take control of the situation. Solutions exist for those who seek answers.

Taking control does not guarantee a reduction in problems. Challenges and obstacles occur for all people, no matter what path is taken. However, the ability to handle difficult situations improves with a good attitude and a purpose in life. Like a knight riding into battle, we are armed for success. We notice opportunities and solutions more readily and are not so easily frightened by obstacles.

To break out of mediocrity and live a full, worthwhile life, we need to acquire the five Keys of overcoming. These Keys work in conjunction with one another to unlock the secrets of personal success. We must master all five elements if the formula is to work properly. There is no one Key to true success!

It is said that success is a journey not a destination. We will not master these Keys before we begin our quest but rather learn as we pursue our goals and dreams. It is this growth that truly enriches our lives. And since the ultimate destination is the end of our earthly life, we possess ample time to master each Key!

Thus begins our journey...

Key 1

Develop a Positive Attitude

[handwritten: Things we can control]

Life is full of uncertainty. There are few things in life we can truly control. We cannot control our environment or the challenges we may face. We certainly can't control other people and what they may say or do.

However, there is one thing we can control- our attitude. How we respond to situations and people is the only thing we can truly master. Almost every outcome and end result will be determined by our attitude. *[handwritten: positive attitude]* A negative attitude will only hold us hostage, but our chances for success and happiness increase with a positive attitude. To transform our world, we must adopt this outlook on life.

Which leads us to the very first Key- develop a positive attitude!

2

Determine the Real Problem

Attitude determines our path in life. It affects every aspect of our personality, our relationships, and our work. How we handle life's occurrences, those little speed bumps in the road, is even more vital than the situation itself. Our reactions reveal our true character.

Attitude is how we view the world, our mental posture. Do we expect the best or the worst? Do we respond negatively or positively? Our attitude will determine our level of success in life, so cultivating a healthy position is crucial.

The difference between a good attitude and a poor attitude is painfully obvious when analyzed. On one side of the coin reside optimism, expectation, and joy. On the other side dwell pessimism, defeat, and misery. These polar opposites are easily revealed, and within seconds of meeting a person, you'll know his attitude. If you inquire about tomorrow's weather, a positive man will say, "It's supposed to rain, which will help the farmers." However, the person with a negative attitude will declare, "It's supposed to be wet and miserable." Same predictions, different attitudes!

No one's life is trouble-free. We all experience set backs and disappointments, and I'm not suggesting there is way in which to prevent such occurrences. However, if our path in life is indeed determined by our attitude, what does this tell us? The problem does not lie with our situations. The real problem is our attitude toward these challenges.

Now, you might refute that statement. You could claim the problem lies with the car that refuses to start or the promotion awarded to another. Answer this question, though. How did you handle the situation? Did you grow frustrated or angry? Did you blame someone else for your misfortune? Or did you seek a solution or make arrangements to avoid that situation in the future?

A positive attitude seeks to move forward while a negative attitude refuses to budge, remaining stuck as if mired in mud. Once stalled, we tend to wallow in self-pity and allow the incident to ruin our whole day. Do not allow this to happen! Pigs wallow, not people. You will only hurt yourself in the process and accomplish nothing.

You cannot control that flat tire or the rude salesman, but you can master your attitude regarding the situation. It's the only thing you can control! Why surrender your one and only power to outside circumstances and other people? Your attitude is your one true possession.

Happiness is a choice. We choose to feel joyful or to feel miserable. When things go wrong, (or at least not according to plan), we are given the opportunity to decide how the situation will affect us. If we refuse to let circumstances dictate our attitude, then they have no real control over our lives. We become the master of our destiny. This is tremendous news indeed!

Your attitude also has a strong impact on your self-image. If your view of the world is negative, then that scrutiny is compounded when turned inward. You cannot expect the worst from others and still truly believe in yourself. A poor attitude is consistent across the board, even in those who appear to despise others but extol their own abilities. They simply do not reveal the negative feelings toward themselves.

What happens to self-esteem when coupled with a negative attitude? Unfortunately, one of life's truths is that you are what you think. The mind's image of oneself becomes the truth. If you maintain an attitude of defeat and doubt in your abilities, this self-portrait will be your reality. You'll believe you don't deserve or cannot accomplish greater things. Sadly, you will be quite correct in this assessment! With a negative attitude, you sabotage your chances for success before you even begin.

How many great people, capable of amazing discoveries and accomplishments, lie hidden behind a poor attitude? How many lives could be affected if they only saw the best in themselves? The poor kid from the wrong side of the tracks who cannot imagine his life ever improving is allowing a negative attitude to control his destiny. He believes he'll remain there forever and that belief will, in turn, be his reality. Such a waste!

Your attitude doesn't just affect your viewpoint. If you maintain a low opinion of yourself, then so will everyone who comes in contact with you. Those in sports and other forms of competition claim they can smell defeat on an opponent. A negative attitude seems to exude as if it were a cloud hanging over one's head. It's also apparent in mannerisms and behavior. Others sense this negative self-image and respond accordingly. They accept at face value the image projected. If you think little of yourself, then so will others!

Not only do we reveal our attitudes to other people, but we influence them as well. Approach wearing a poor attitude and the other person will mirror similar feelings. Proportionately, negative is a stronger force than positive, and thus a much greater influence. So it comes as no surprise that a poor state of mind will likely overwhelm a good attitude. Consider this fact the next time you encounter a negative person. Was his poor attitude simply a reflection of yours?

Attitudes are similar to magnets. Just as metal is drawn to a strong magnet, positive attitudes attract. Those possessing optimism will naturally pull together and find strength and support in numbers. Negative attitudes tend to group together as well, feeding off one anther's pessimism. However, like water and oil, the two groups do not mix well!

When positive people (and those residing someplace in between) encounter a negative attitude, they are instantly repelled. Consider the last time you came across one of these doom and gloom types. You seized the first opportunity to escape that person's presence, didn't you? There's an expression that states a winner cannot stand a loser. Those with optimistic attitudes will not associate for long with pessimistic people. If they do, then they run the risk of becoming just like them!

Now that you understand the power of one's attitude and its role in daily life, the importance of a positive attitude becomes very apparent. We can blame circumstances, but ultimately, it is our attitude that determines our fate. A positive outlook not only increases our chances for success, but it makes life's journey much more pleasant!

In a nutshell...
- Attitude is how we view the world
- The real problem is one's own attitude
- Happiness and misery are both choices
- Your attitude affects your self-image
- People respond in kind to our attitudes
- Positive attracts while negative repels

3

Aspects and Developing a PMA

You have probably heard the phrase "positive mental attitude," or PMA for short, quite often. Its importance is constantly touted, and yet, few of us ever take a class on the subject. Even those who understand the concept rarely apply it to their lives. Just what is this mysterious PMA and how can we use it to better ourselves?

First, we must understand the difference between a positive and a negative mental attitude. They are as different as day and night; hot and cold; good and evil. Once you grasp the dissimilarity, these two attitudes become very easy to spot in others. So, what are the basic characteristics?

A positive attitude is belief that success can be achieved by employing optimism. It embodies happiness, honesty and peace. It results in constant activity and the pursuit of better circumstances. Like the flower's nectar attracts the bees, a positive attitude attracts others.

As one can well imagine, a negative attitude expresses the very opposite. It is filled with misery, dishonesty and discord. Instead of activity, it tends to remain fixed, and the lack of movement means wallowing in circumstances.

Since a positive attitude is optimistic and expects the best, it is often dismissed as unrealistic. However, nothing could be further from the truth! Our self-images are determined by our beliefs and expectations, and so is the reality in which we exist. Yes, circumstances arise that are beyond our control. Our positive or negative attitudes influence the occurrence of these situations and determine the outcome more often than we think. We don't always get what we want, but we usually get what we expect.

Still not convinced? Consider people for whom everything appears to go wrong. They seem to actually attract problems! They expect negative situations and are rarely disappointed when life constantly hands them lemons. Possessing a negative attitude, they convince themselves that nothing will ever go right, either. What they do not realize is the human mind is powerful indeed, and their brain goes to great lengths to validate their beliefs. It helps to form the negative atmosphere in which they live.

"Believing in yourself is the key to success. It starts with saying you can."
- Lynn Tincher, author of Afterthoughts
www.lynntincher.com

It's not just negative situations they attract, either. Those of similar mindset usually surround a person with a poor attitude. This compounds the negativity, prompting even more misery and inactivity. Picture a bucket full of crabs, all pulling one another down, and you get the idea. With friends and associates like that, no wonder the negative person never gets ahead!

So how does one cultivate a positive mental attitude? First on the list is to develop some optimism. No one has achieved success without it! Optimism is looking past obstacles and refusing to accept them as facts. It is seeking another path, a better route, and not resigning to circumstances as if they were fate.

At the very core of optimism is hope and faith. Think of all the great inventions and discoveries that can be credited to optimistic belief! The Wright brothers were convinced man could fly. Ford believed he could build a machine that would be better than a horse and buggy. And, even after ten thousand unsuccessful attempts, Edison still believed the light bulb would work! All of these men continued to move forward because they were optimistic of success. They did not give up because they expected victory at some point.

Are you anticipating and experiencing positive triumphs in your life? Or are you experiencing negative setbacks? If, in life, we get what we expect, then obviously you need to raise your expectations. When you arise in the morning, do you foresee a great day or a bad day? Expecting a lousy day automatically places you on the defense, and you subconsciously seek negative experiences. You will project that negative onto every situation and person that crosses your path, and life has a way of responding accordingly.

Perhaps an example would clarify the difference between positive and negative expectations. Suppose you walked into a room carrying a basketful of puppies. What reaction would you predict from those gathered? With the exception of someone who fears dogs, you would expect everyone to crowd around the basket. You are in essence coming at them with a positive attitude and high expectations.

However, what if you walked into that room with a basket filled with cobras? It's a pretty safe bet you would clear the room! Those threatening cobras are a perfect representation of a negative attitude. You would expect and receive a negative reaction.

Instead of anticipating and seeking the negative, try raising your expectations. Leave the bad attitude, and the cobras, at home! Approach the day anticipating great things. Expect to perform better at your job or during recreational activities. Believe you will encounter pleasant people. Be on the watch for opportunities. You may not succeed on every level or in all situations. However, you stand a better chance armed with a positive attitude than a basket of poisonous snakes.

What else is required for a positive mental attitude? You must possess enthusiasm and excitement. I call it spunk! There is no spirit more powerful or energetic. It is difficult to remain negative when you are full of eager exuberance. Spirited enthusiasm will supply you with energy and endurance. It requires effort, but once impassioned, your excitement will continue to feed itself.

But what happens if this does not come natural for you? What do you do when you don't feel enthusiastic? There is an expression that claims you should 'fake it until you make it'. Enthusiasm doesn't just happen on its own- you must make it happen! Turn the passion and excitement up a couple notches and energize your thoughts. Act as if you possess enthusiasm, and pretty soon, you'll feel it as well. You will soon discover that the energy required for negativity and pessimism is actually greater. Once optimistic enthusiasm takes over, the sensation is empowering!

There is another critical part of the equation. You must eliminate negative thoughts from your mind. Our brains are constant chatterboxes, barraging us with a never-ending stream of images, words and feelings. Unfortunately for most of us, this babble tends to be negative in nature. To make matters worse, a good portion of this we direct at ourselves. It is difficult to maintain a great attitude while being beaten up from within!

Stop acting as if you are your own worst enemy! Learn to curtail this constant flow of negative assessment. Eliminate words such as "can't," "failure," and "stupid" from your vocabulary, spoken and unspoken. Control the tone of your inner voice and be aware of doubt and discouragement entering your thoughts. If you discover negativity creeping in now and then, simply redirect your thoughts. You are what you think, so think good things about yourself.

OVERCOMING

"The first step to developing a positive attitude is to resist illicit thoughts! Thoughts that are harmful to us and others. Thoughts that leave us frustrated and discouraged. Thoughts that make us feel fearful and intimidated. Thoughts that put us on a guilt trip. Thoughts that leave us feeling inferior. All of these are examples of thinking that must be cast down and cast out."
- Bill Wilson, author & Pastor of The Lord's Table

OBSTACLES

By employing optimism and enthusiasm, raising expectations, and eliminating negative thoughts, we will discover a positive attitude that is ready to flourish and grow. It is doubtful this transformation will take place overnight, so be prepared. Time is required to form any habit and a positive attitude is no exception to this rule. As changes begin to occur, we come to recognize moments of negativity and can steer away from such thoughts and behaviors. The effort is well worth the rewards, too!

A positive mental attitude views the world with fresh eyes. It appreciates every moment and attacks life with boundless energy and spirit. Charge your attitude with optimism and prepare for great things to occur!

In a nutshell...
- A positive attitude implies optimism, joy and activity
- A negative attitude implies pessimism, misery and inactivity
- We get what we expect
- Develop optimism and belief
- Act with enthusiasm
- Eliminate negative thoughts

4

Proactive Not Reactive

Every motivational speaker and self-help book touts the virtues of being proactive. What exactly does it mean to be proactive? What is the mystique surrounding this word?

Proactive puts you in control. No matter how the scenario unfolds, whether for better or for worse, you are the master. This does not imply you can control the conditions or even the final outcome. However, the circumstances will not control you. More specifically, they will not control your attitude or behavior.

This is yet another important component of a positive mental attitude. A proactive person will not allow situations to control his actions. He is in full control of his attitude and can make decisions independently of the circumstances. Behavior and response will not be based on the crisis of the moment, nor determined by outside influences.

It goes beyond just handling a given situation. A proactive person is ready for problems before they even occur. He anticipates a challenge and prepares in advance. This should not be confused with a negative attitude, though. A negative attitude expects problems but does not possess solutions. A proactive person expects the best but is prepared should plans go awry.

Just as a positive attitude focuses on moving forward, so proactive possesses the same drive and motivation. Prepared for problems, a proactive individual has no difficulty taking the initiative. If he desires to remain in control, he will need to make the first move. It is much easier to go on the offense than be forced to play defense!

Responsibility plays a key role as well. We are often told to stand up and take responsibility for our lives. The proactive person embodies this trait through wisdom, foresight, and maturity. He understands that he cannot blame circumstances. If he's really in control, then whatever the consequences of his actions, the blame or credit falls squarely in his lap. He takes full responsibility for his actions and behavior.

At the opposite end of the spectrum is reactivity. Often we call it reacting without thinking, and that is a fair assessment! A reactive person responds emotionally and quickly rather than carefully thinking through the situation. Lacking a plan, his snap judgment occasionally results in poor decisions.

Reacting turns control over to the circumstances. Instead of mastering the situation, one surrenders to outside forces. Once control has been relinquished, that person is at the mercy of his environment and must accept the fate dealt by life. He is a leaf on the wind, caught in a violent thunderstorm and feeling quite helpless.

By refusing to take control, a reactive person also refuses to assume responsibility. He claims he is the victim of circumstances. He cannot be held accountable for his misfortunes! Unfortunately, once a person places blame elsewhere, he ceases to seek a solution to his problems. That individual believes that since life dealt this fate, it can provide the solution as well. He will stubbornly sit and wait for answers, helplessly wallowing in negative thoughts and self-pity.

If reacting renders us powerless, why would anyone choose this path? Is it really easier to relinquish control and wash our hands of all responsibility?

It might appear easier, but it is not natural. Human nature is actually proactive because it promotes growth and balance. Reacting tends to stagnate people, but nothing in nature is stagnant. All things constantly grow and change, from the flower than blooms and dies to the rock worn by rushing waters. When we go against this force, we become out of sync with life. Nature demands that we change and grow, and we achieve this through proactive behavior.

Remember, it is not just positive thinking! Just as knowledge is power only when applied, so proactive requires more than just optimistic thoughts. Problems won't go away just because you believe. You must face the reality of your situation, formulate a solution, and then act on that plan.

Let's provide an example. Suppose you were laid off from work? *Example's* If you were to spend the next week complaining to family and friends how you were wronged, that would be considered a reactive response. You have chosen to do nothing but blame your circumstances. However, if you were to immediately set out to find employment elsewhere, that would be a proactive response. You have focused on a solution rather than the problem.

The ability to maintain grace under pressure is a proactive characteristic. When problems arise, a proactive person does not panic. He maintains his calm demeanor and is not rattled when things do not go according to plan. This does not mean he feels no frustration. He simply does not dwell on those negative feelings and thoughts. Seizing the initiative, he pursues a solution instead.

We've all seen the opposite reaction, though. Like a chicken with its head cut off, that person can only run in circles! Little is accomplished when an individual allows his emotions to take control. The energy required for a panic attack would be better utilized pursuing a solution.

Proactive behavior is a choice. Begin conditioning your responses today. In life, you are either the horse or the rider. Take control of your situations or they will control you!

In a nutshell...
- Proactive behavior puts you in control
- A proactive individual is responsible and ready for problems
- Reacting hands control over to outside forces
- Humans are naturally proactive
- Maintain grace under pressure

5

Associations

Our associations affect our behavior and mental state far more than we realize. People tend to take on the attributes of those around them, for better or for worse. The secret is to form associations that are a positive influence on our lives and not a negative drain.

Most people were told by their mothers not to hang out with certain kids because they were a bad influence. Amazingly, we forget this advice when we become adults. We often select friends and associates who are less than positive and display destructive tendencies. However, the rules of association still apply and we are affected by these influences.

Association is a powerful force and can shape one's thoughts and behaviors. If you doubt this force, consider the outcome of the abandoned puppy placed with a litter of kittens. Surrounded by felines, he will grow up thinking he is a cat! That puppy will simply not realize he is a dog. The other living creatures in his environment influence his behavior more than any other force or condition.

Fortunately, humans are a little more sophisticated and intelligent. We can fall victim to such extremes, though, as evidenced by brainwashing and other forms of mental programming. Children are especially susceptible to such influences. Most of us will never experience such tactics or allow them to be performed on our person. However, we consciously permit associations to affect our lives every day, either through subtle persuasion or conformation.

Creatures of habit, we are drawn to familiar territory. We seek those who match our moral standards, economic status, and ambition levels. Consider those within your own circle of influence and you will discover they are your associates because you are comfortable in their presence. Occasionally we will be forced to stretch or shrink to fit our environment. Like the chameleon, we change our colors just enough to blend.

Your associations determine your placement in life. You will never outgrow your surroundings. The goldfish in a small fishbowl will only grow so large, but place him in a twenty-gallon tank and his size will increase to match his living quarters. Our associations influence us much like the goldfish's tank, either by encouraging or restricting our growth.

Now, I am not suggesting that you need to make all new friends. (And you certainly cannot trade in your family members, no matter how hard you try!) However, if you possess far more drive and ambition than your circle of influence, then that is a problem. You must have someone who will push you to greater heights. The tennis player who can beat everyone at the country club will never improve further until he plays outside of this small group. We must also step outside of our comfort zones if we expect to achieve more and grow as individuals.

Separate yourself from those who wallow in mediocrity. Avoid individuals who possess negative attitudes and aren't afraid to show it. Distance yourself from those with potentially destructive behaviors and habits. Retreat from the underachievers and pessimists in life. Not only will these types of people hinder your efforts to grow and succeed, they will also resent your ambition and attempt to dampen your spirits. You do not need friends like that in your corner.

Instead, seek individuals who are actively pursuing ambitions and goals. Befriend those possessing positive attitudes and who are moving forward in life or already possess a measure of success. They will encourage and stretch you. It is likely they will be in a position where they can apply direct influence as well. Certainly, they will be more willing to offer advice and help you achieve your goals.

Get a mentor

In your quest for support and guidance, you would do well to cultivate a mentor. Select an individual who has traveled your path of choice and achieved success. This person can assist you in numerous ways, probably beyond what you dreamed possible. He can help formulate a plan, warn you of the pitfalls, provide encouragement, and introduce you to others of influence. Your chances for success increase dramatically with a mentor's careful guidance. After all, would you prefer to go through the minefield alone or follow someone who can advise you where to step?

How does one find a mentor? They are not sold in stores, but potential mentors reside closer than you think! Begin by observing the leaders in your field. Is there someone in particular that you admire and can easily access? Approach this individual and ask for a moment of his time or perhaps take him to lunch. Express your admiration and respect before seeking his advice, or you will appear very self-serving. Your goal is to build a lasting relationship, not just pump that person for information. Your mentor may become your greatest ally and friend if you honor and respect him. And of course, if you follow his wisdom and advice!

be willing to help others

Once we begin to achieve success, we will discover others now seeking our assistance. Just as we benefited from those in a position to help us, so should we be willing to extend our hand as well. Be willing to assist others up the ladder of success. Not only will we benefit from these relationships and further expand our network, we also continue to learn in the role of teacher.

The days of apprenticeship, where a master taught his young pupil valuable skills in a trade or craft, are long gone. We have lost so many great benefits that were provided through such relationships. The impact of a mentor is very powerful, so do not falter in your quest to locate such an individual. His influence will create a lasting impact on your life and leave you enriched by his presence.

Associations are incredibly important and can determine our success or failure in life. Do not allow personal contacts to influence or control your life in a negative manner. Surround yourself with successful encouragers and watch your world be forever transformed!

In a nutshell...
- Association is a powerful force
- We associate with those who make us feel comfortable
- You will never outgrow your surroundings
- Separate yourself from mediocrity
- Find a mentor
- Guide others on their path

6

Integrity and Honesty

Integrity and honesty form the basic foundation of all relationships. Remove these traits and friendships quickly die and organizations crumble. Even in a society where standards are gradually decreasing, the consequences of failing to adhere to these principals become readily apparent. More than ever, a man's reputation is still tied to these values.

It comes as no surprise that honesty, integrity, and honor are mentioned almost four hundred times in the Bible. Obviously, there is a premium on these qualities. If we possess no honor and cannot be trusted, we receive no support and our allies flee. A dishonest man finds himself cut off from others and truly alone in the world. Imagine if society as a whole dropped integrity and honesty by the wayside. It would result in utter chaos!

Author C. Denise Sutton has this to say about honesty and integrity:

Webster defines integrity as 'a conduct that conforms to an accepted standard of right and wrong', 'devotion to telling the truth', and 'faithfulness to high moral standards.' So, how important are integrity and honesty in building a positive mental attitude and strong leadership skills? Your answer lies within the following scenarios. First, think of a person who has been very honest with you, especially when it would have been easier for him or her to be dishonest. Then, think of a person who was dishonest with you whom you felt would have received much more

34

cooperation from you by being honest. What are your personal feelings about each person? What did you tell others about these persons? How quick would you do business or 'make a deal' with either person in the future?

Now, think of some times that you were dishonest in the past. How did it make you feel? How did others respond to your lack of integrity? Now, think of those times that you were honest and how it made you feel, even if the other person did not know or believe that you were honest?

Honesty and integrity go far in building strong business and personal relationships and in helping a person feel better about him or herself in the process. We now live in an era in which success is often defined by material wealth, yet an honorable reputation can, in the end, be the key to bringing a person the contentment he seeks in accomplishing his or her life or company goals. Think of the chaos that would occur if coworkers were afraid to relay vital information or place important projects into the hands of those they felt would abuse it in some way. This would lead to a breakdown in interoffice communication and production.

True leaders must work on the basis of knowing that nothing compares to an honorable reputation and, in turn, strive to instill these ideas in his or her followers in order to build strong teams within the organization. This leader's honesty must show up in his personal, as well as his business life, so that there will be no confusion from onlookers where this person morally stands. This person must understand that his or her company is not there to be served but is there to serve others. A company's reputation is built on that of its employees and a name that takes years to build can be destroyed in a matter of seconds. Therefore, any decision made should be based on honesty and integrity.

For more insight on this, go to C. Denise Sutton's article "The Name Game" at www.mywordsandme.com.

Consistency is the key. One must remain honest and true in all areas of life. Once deceit creeps into any aspect of a person's world, then he can no longer be trusted on any level. The man who claims to conduct business honestly but is engaged in an affair on his wife is living a double standard that only he believes. If the truth of his personal life is revealed, his business dealings will be questioned as well. Truly honest people apply this trait across the board and possess no reason to lie under any circumstance.

In addition to maintaining consistency, our motives should be pure. Honor and integrity imply that we are not focused solely on our own needs, desires and ambitions. A self-serving attitude will quickly reveal itself to others. We soon discover no one trusts us to accurately represent his or her interests. This is detrimental to business dynamics. Without trust, our subordinates will not follow or support us. In the personal realm, it can end relationships completely.

Both in business and in pleasure, we are judged by the company we keep. Employees become ambassadors for a business and represent our company's ethical standards and practices. Therefore, a leader must instill the traits of honor and integrity in his followers as well. Just as honesty needs to be consistent in an individual, so should that trait be displayed in every aspect of an organization.

Consider the leaders who have fallen due to a traitor or a dishonest follower, and you will understand the importance of mutual integrity. Set the example early. Do not reward any underhanded dealings, regardless of the subsequent rewards. Encourage your people to act honestly and with honor in all situations. Keeping up with your own lies is difficult enough without taking on the deceptions of your entire organization.

Never falter in your adherence to the principals of honor and honesty. All that is required is one slip of character, one moment of unfaithfulness, or one simple lie to destroy a man's reputation. Sugar cubes dissolve instantly in boiling water. So will your reputation if you are caught fabricating the truth! What took years to create will not only vanish in an instant, but will become nearly impossible to rebuild. Consider the man who is sent to prison for a crime. That moment of complete lack of judgment will follow him for a very long time.

Honor and integrity are modified by society's standards and the personal values we uphold. How others view us is a direct reflection of our ability to adhere to these expectations. Deviations from these standards tend to compound and eventually dishonesty catches up to us. If we are honest in all things, then we

36

do not fear repercussions from contradicting a lie. That means less on which to worry!

Reputation is one of the most valuable intangibles a man can possess. Remain honest and true, and you will never have to worry that such a prized asset might be lost.

In a nutshell...
- A dishonest man is alone in the world
- Integrity is conforming to standards of right and wrong
- You must be consistent in your dealings
- Instill honesty in your followers as well
- Reputation is gained slowly, lost instantly

7

Team Membership
and the Proper Work Ethic

"Be a team player!" How many times have you heard or seen that particular slogan? However, there are some great principles and work ethics behind this overused phrase. We would benefit by adopting some of those values and applying the positive attitude and behaviors that accompany those traits.

The goal of a team player is to help everyone succeed as a whole. Notice it does not imply simply achieving one's own personal ambitions. Individual aims will be realized along the way, but these are not the ultimate destination of the team. Our focus must be on the group if the primary goals are to be accomplished.

Pastor and author, Bill Wilson, offers these thoughts on becoming a team member:

Without the team players on the team, you don't have a team.
- You have a bunch of individuals crowded together.

A team player always tries to consider the big picture.
- Just being concerned with your own needs will make you petty.

A team player will encourage more than criticize.
- The old saying... it's better to light a candle than curse the dark is still true!

The team player understands that unity produces power.
- The law of Synergism...

- It is two or more agents working together to produce a result not obtainable by any of the agents independently.
- Synergy or synergism comes from two Greek words: erg, meaning 'to work', and syn, meaning 'together'; hence, synergism is 'working together'.

Geese fly in a "V" formation, proving the law of Synergism.

- The front wings of the lead geese create upward air current so powerful that when flying together they can fly 71% further than when alone.

T- ogether
E- ach
A- ccomplishes
M- ore
- *Bill Wilson, author & Pastor of The Lord's Table*

A positive attitude is a helpful attitude. For the good of the whole, we must assist those around us. Offer to help complete their tasks and give support and encouragement. A rising tide lifts all ships and elevating others accomplishes a common goal. A helpful attitude is effective whether we are one of the workers or the leader, as well. We should offer assistance regardless of our position.

OVERCOMING

"Sometimes it's hard to remember that whatever benefits the group benefits you. I find that selfishness is my natural tendency, so I've developed a philosophy I call enlightened self-interest. That means I accept the truth that whatever benefits the group most also benefits me. For example, serving as an officer in a writer's club and arranging good events for all has raised my status in the writing community, and promoting other people's work has caused others to promote me. Working hard for any group you belong to is always more beneficial than the same amount of work for yourself."
- *Austin S. Camacho, author of the Hannibal Jones Mysteries*
www.ascamacho.com

Performing one's assigned duties and functioning as a team player is difficult without clear instructions. Be sure others understand their positions and obligations. If we are the one in charge, then we must be certain the workers know what is expected of them. Often job descriptions and job expectations do not coincide one hundred percent! If expectations are not clearly defined, a person may miss the mark even though he is performing his assignments correctly. Set a standard and communicate desires. Once he's been informed of expectations, that person will do everything possible to successfully meet our needs and goals.

Occasionally the leader feels he is the only capable person. Micro-managing only accomplishes two things- it fills the leader's time with unnecessary busy-work and it restricts the subordinate's abilities. (Not to mention it annoys them as well!) Encourage and empower people to work on their own. It will build their confidence, increase productivity and inspire the pursuit of new ideas. If we are not in a position of leadership, then we must demonstrate to our superiors that we are capable of working independently.

In addition to empowering individuals to work on their own, bestow on them specific duties and responsibilities. If you want to determine who works best without supervision or are seeking leaders within the group, this is an excellent manner in which to accomplish those tasks. Select people who appear to crave responsibility and thrive on challenges. Once you have granted them an assignment, step aside and observe what they manage to accomplish for the good of the organization.

Occasionally you will come across someone who is not a good team player or potential leader. He may be a good person but just falls short of expectations or fails to act appropriately within a reasonable period. Discuss the matter with him and provide a little guidance or additional time. If that individual still cannot accomplish his goals, then you may need to ease him out of that particular position. Do so gradually so as to maintain a positive atmosphere while not destroying his confidence. This may not be a pleasant experience or viewed as a favorable move. However, if he has failed to perform for the good of the team, then you must be willing to act responsibly.

Holding our subordinates accountable to standards applies to us as well! Regardless of rank, placement or position, every individual needs to answer to another person. Those below us should also have to answer to one another. True teamwork implies that everyone is accountable. These checks and balances will keep the organization running smoothly.

Proper work ethic implies that we should display all of the qualities we want our people to possess. As a leader, we should work harder and encourage more often than anyone else in the organization. We must set the example and achieve results, not just activity. Followers will emulate our bad traits faster than our good traits, so provide them with as few negative habits as possible!

If this sounds like hard labor, remember this final word of advice. Sometimes the best work is completed while having fun. Yes, you read that correctly! Encourage others to enjoy the working experience. When a job or duty becomes a source of misery or boredom, workers grow restless and productivity slides. Invigorate the environment with a little relaxing fun. It will increase morale, provide an opportunity to release some steam, and increase the flow of work. So, let your people have some fun once in a while!

A team member is a multi-faceted and complex individual. However, the qualities are not difficult to achieve. Focus on the goals of the team, support each individual component, and remember that Together Everyone Achieves More!

In a nutshell...
- Help the team succeed as a whole
- Remember the law of synergism
- Be sure each person understands his duties
- Empower individuals to work independently
- Everyone is accountable to someone
- Don't forget to have fun!

8

Problems and a PMA

So far, the first Key has focused on a positive attitude. Why then does this final section deal with problems? Because problems continue to happen regardless! It is only by employing a positive attitude that we successfully handle the negative aspects of these challenges.

If possessing a good attitude attracts positive, why do problems continue to occur? As a Christian, I personally believe there is an evil force controlling life on earth that delights in creating problems for everyone. Regardless of what you may believe, we can chalk it up to the fact that life is not perfect. Despite a positive attitude, high expectations, and careful planning, some things simply go wrong without rhyme or reason. Life is not fair. The sooner we realize this truth, the sooner we can move forward.

Even if you possess a positive outlook, there will be times when barriers arise to thwart your progress. These obstacles and delays are frustrating. It is perfectly acceptable to feel frustrated, though. Since emotions in of themselves are not wrong, and we are only human, we all feel discouraged and baffled now and then. Short-term frustration happens to the best of us.

The real trouble begins when we allow frustration to stop us in our tracks, though. A moment's pause as we regroup and form a proactive resolution is acceptable. Unfortunately, too many people allow their frustrations to halt all forward progress. Feeling defeated, these individuals lose sight of their goals and slip into depression. Do not fall into this trap! Remove your eyes from the obstacle, refocus on your destination, and do not give in to the urge to quit.

Problematic situations reveal one's true character. When life throws a curve ball, it's imperative that we maintain an even temper in the face of adversity. Regardless of how we feel, we need to prevent our emotions from bubbling over in a froth of unpredictability. We all know individuals who wear their hearts on their sleeves. Unsure of their mood, we are often forced to walk on eggshells in their presence. Do not join their ranks by allowing life's little uncertainties to severely disrupt your emotional stability.

We tend to want to share our misery when problems occur as well. Sometimes discussing a situation with another human being will make us feel better. However, unloading our burdens on every unsuspecting victim does not cause those people to feel better and certainly doesn't add to our popularity. Every group has a 'Gloomy Gus' who whines constantly about his problems, and no one enjoys his company for this very reason. Take care you do not become this individual! We all need a confidant, but dumping on everyone we encounter will not solve our problems.

Overwhelmed by troubles, it may feel tempting to play the blame game. My problems are everyone's fault but my own! This reactive response is incredibly negative and self-defeating, not to mention incredibly immature. Take responsibility for your own life and avoid blaming other people or the circumstances. Even if another person is the cause of your sorrows, you will accomplish nothing by assigning blame. If that individual caused the problem, you can bet he will not provide a solution! Suck it up and find your own answers.

Problems are incredibly discouraging when it appears the path is completely blocked. Every goal or ambition boasts many trails leading to its attainment, though. How many times have we heard that when one door shuts, another will open? Almost to the point of annoyance? Yet, there is great truth in that statement. It basically means that an alternate route to our final destination exists if we do not abandon our quest. After all, few ventures proceed exactly as originally planned. Columbus was seeking another route to India. He eventually accomplished this goal, but not without discovering America first. Talk about a situation not proceeding according to plan!

If the idea of your carefully planned route abruptly colliding with a brick wall disturbs and frightens you, then broaden your view on the situation. There are many opportunities for success open to those who possess optimism and determination. If there's more than one way to skin a cat, then there's certainly another means by which to overcome your obstacles. Employ a little optimism when facing your challenges. Go over, tunnel underneath, or simply batter that wall in front of you!

When all else fails and you are faced with an impossible situation, you simply need to trust and believe circumstances will improve. It requires a measure of faith on your part, especially when there is no evidence. This is the true test of a positive attitude. Cling to hope and stay focused on the goal. Proverbs 29:18 states 'Where there is no vision, the people perish...' Without hope and belief, you will not succeed. Control all within your capability to master and do not allow your attitude to slide into despair.

Problems appear and disappear, but they should not shake your life's very foundation. A positive attitude is far more important and certainly stronger than any negative situation. Do not allow troubles to disrupt your journey to success. Focus on your goals and no obstacle will possess the power to remain in your path!

In a nutshell...
- Problems will continue to occur
- Do not allow frustration to stop you
- Maintain an even disposition
- Avoid the blame game
- More than one path always exists
- Do not lose hope or belief

Key 2

People Skills

The most important trait you can develop is skill with people. The great Andrew Carnegie claimed he valued an employee who worked well with others over all else. If a billionaire believed people skills were that essential, then perhaps we should work on fine-tuning those skills!

Sadly, the ability to get along with others is not taught in school. We know how to add and read, but we don't know how to deal with the masses. What we learn occurs mostly through trial and error. Many never even grasp the concept. If we want to succeed in life, though, we must be able to properly interact with other human beings.

Which brings us to the second Key- people skills!

9

Understanding Basic Truths

Before we can begin acquiring people skills, there are a few basic truths that must be grasped. Understanding human nature is critical and provides a foundation on which to build. Without that foundation, our house of skills will crumble and fall.

One of the most basic human truths stems from our selfish nature. Our primary concern and focus in life is ourselves! Whether due to our strong spirit or our self-preservation instincts, we place ourselves about all other considerations. We are the center of our own universe and more important than anyone else.

Understandably, we are our favorite topic as well. We know more about our lives than any other subject. We are cognizant of the details and struggles of our daily existence- the hopes and dreams, the beliefs and desires, the feelings, and the forces that come against us. It is a subject of which we never tire, either. Despite our failings in other areas, it will always be the one region where we are the experts.

We want others to know about us, too. We find joy in sharing our lives with another human being. The artist who has just completed his master creation will eagerly share with you his great accomplishment. The new grandmother will proudly speak of her grandchild. And the young lady who just received a proposal of marriage will want to tell the whole world!

This self-fascination leads into another basic truth. We all crave approval. We long to hear that we are accepted and liked by others. When another human being pays attention and truly listens to us, it conveys a sense of importance. Our sense of worth either increases from their interest or is reduced by their rejection. Sometimes we even resort to negative and destructive behavior to elicit a response that will justify our existence. The desire for acceptance factors into almost everything we do or say.

This constant need for approval is either adequately met or goes unfulfilled, thus affecting a person's self esteem. Whether positive or negative, we all carry within us a unique self-image- a perceived value of ourselves. The manner in which we react to people and situations depends on our level of self-esteem and how well we truly respect ourselves. Our belief in others starts with believing in ourselves first.

Those who feel unworthy or unimportant slowly develop a poor self-image. The person who puts others down to make himself feel better and the shy person who hides in his shell both suffer from low self-esteem. Their ego is starved for approval and yet feels threatened by others, literally placing them between a rock and a hard place. Approaching those with a low self-image can be difficult, although not impossible if done with care and determination.

A person with a high self-esteem will not feel intimidated by other people. He can be approached with ease and confidence. An occasional lack of acceptance or a criticism does not threaten his entire existence. His ego can still be bruised, but he will bounce back from the experience.

Despite this self-image disparity, you still do not want to hurt a person's ego. No one enjoys verbal assaults on the self-worth. Treat others with the same respect and interest you want to receive. Your words and actions must be genuine, though. Concern, intrigue and belief cannot be faked without appearing shallow and self-serving.

This leads to another important facet in human behavior- the mirror effect. People will respond to you as if they were peering into a looking glass. Your mood, positive or negative, becomes the reflection and they react in a similar fashion. Our defenses naturally rise and fall with every encounter, depending on the emotional state of the people we meet. A man approached in anger will almost always grow angry as well, but when confronted with kindness, he will become friendly.

Understanding of this mirror effect works to your advantage. It eliminates the fear associated with approaching people, because if you act in a positive manner, you almost guarantee they will respond in a similar fashion. Pleasantries and courtesy go a long way, as will a genuine smile. Try this approach for one week and see if your encounters do not improve in quality!

If knowing that people value themselves most, crave approval, respond to you in kind, and that humans possess sensitive self-images, then it stands to reason effort will be required on your part! The same qualities reside within you and those needs must be met as well. However, a miraculous thing happens when you focus on others- you find the gesture is reciprocated. Your appreciation and belief in other people will be returned. You cannot give expecting to receive, though. The desire to fulfill other people's needs must be genuine.

Once you understand these basic human truths, you are on your way to mastering people skills.

In a nutshell...
- A person's favorite topic is himself.
- Everyone craves approval.
- Lack of approval results in a poor self-image
- People respond to us as if peering into a mirror
- Never attack a man's ego
- Expect the best and believe in others

10

Understanding Shyness
and Making Contact

One obstacle that occasionally appears between us and other people is shyness. It prevents us from reaching out and connecting with our fellow man in a meaningful fashion. However, we should not allow a demure and timid nature stop us from developing people skills.

Bashful tendencies develop at a very young age and can follow us into adulthood. Childish fears slowly become restrictive inhibitions, causing in us a reluctance to step out of our comfort zones. While cautions should not be thrown to the wind, a wary and fearful attitude prevents us from experiencing people and life to the fullest.

We offer many explanations for our shyness. Some people claim they are simply not the talkative or sociable type. Preference to follow rather than lead is often cited as an excuse. Others describe their bashful nature as a desire to remain out of the limelight and merely watch from the sidelines. Internally, many simply fear they will be disliked or hurt by other people. The reasons vary from one individual to the other.

But what is the real underlying cause? Despite all of these seemingly different excuses, shyness comes from only one thing- a problem with human relations. It is our inability and reluctance to reach out to other people that hold us prisoner.

Shyness is more than just a barrier to enjoying meaningful relationships. It is a wall that separates us from new concepts and experiences. When we cannot access people, we cannot access their ideas, either. It limits how far we can expand our world and confines us to only one way of thinking. In order to continue growing as a person, we must extend our horizons, and this means relating to other people.

First, we must learn to lower our defenses and drop our proverbial shields. Learn to expect a positive reaction from others! Remember the mirror effect- if we are friendly and gracious, the other person will act accordingly. If your encounters tend to be unpleasant, then you have to ask yourself a question. Am I approaching these people with the wrong attitude? Do I present myself as defensive and negative? You may have to make some changes. After all, you can't control the response or reaction of others, but you can control you.

In order to effectively reach out to others, we must remember two things. First, that person in front of us probably feels nervous, too. Second, he is more worried about what we will think of him than vice versa. (And therefore doesn't even notice our apprehension!) He shares our fear of rejection and desire for acceptance, and that individual hopes the encounter will be pleasant as well. Now that we know there is nothing to fear, we can alleviate his anxiety by providing an affirmative response. Not only will our fear vanish but we will both receive a boost to the ego. It's a win-win situation!

Encounters and first contacts should not be frightful or awkward. Here are some tips to help you through:

- Make eye contact with everyone
- Smile pleasantly
- Maintain an open, friendly posture
- Say hello!

If you repeatedly practice these steps with every person who crosses your path, it will soon become second nature. Your attention will shift and you'll begin to notice other people. Instead of rushing through your day, caught up in the confines of your own existence, you will truly see the multitude of fascinating people around you. They will peak your interest rather than instill fear. At this point, your world really expands!

You ask, but what happens if I am forced to interact with these people? This should not be a cause for panic, either! Conversations are easy if you just remember the basic rules of human nature and appeal to those inner motivations.

One thing that will put you ahead of the curve is to speak that individual's name. Once he has introduced himself, repeat the name to be sure you heard it correctly. Use that person's name several times during the course of the conversation. This conveys respect and a sense of importance. Nothing is sweeter than the sound of one's own name!

"I struggle with shyness. I've learned to make small talk with almost everyone I meet. This will help you tackle bigger obstacles later."
- Lynn Tincher, author of Afterthoughts
www.lynntincher.com

Try altering your vocabulary and using the word 'you' instead of 'I.' It shifts the focus from you to the other person. It is nearly impossible to monopolize a conversation without using the word 'I' or 'me!' Not only does this feed his ego, but your nervousness will take a back seat and not draw unwanted attention.

Learn to relax- this is just another human being, just like you. Do not wind yourself so tight that you become unapproachable. As the saying goes, just be yourself. Remain calm but confident and do not try to overcompensate for your feelings of inadequacy. Forced eagerness is just as bad as a timid, fearful approach. We've all encountered people who were trying too hard and their words and actions appeared unnatural. You don't need to drastically alter your personality- just act open, friendly, and true to self.

We cannot break free of shyness overnight. Fortunately, what took years to develop can be reversed in a manner of months if we put forth the effort. And, developing good human relations is the first step!

In a nutshell...
- Shyness is a lack of people skills.
- Shyness cuts us off from people and ideas.
- Expect others to like you.
- Learn to master encounters.
- Show respect by using a person's name.
- Focus on the other person and relax.

11

Listening

We are bombarded every day by thousands of sounds. The constant noise means that we tend to tune out most of what we hear. Unfortunately, this often includes the words of others. But it is when we take the time to listen that we really learn and grow.

People on a whole are truly fascinating. Their experiences are as varied as their shapes, sizes and backgrounds. Even siblings raised under similar circumstances develop different tastes and opinions. There is just so much to learn from others that we would never experience in our own lifetime.

Listening is an art form and a skill. It requires effort to concentrate on something other than our internal voice. Too often, we fail to pay attention to what other people are really saying. This results in a drastic loss of information and poor transfer of ideas. Failure to listen causes conversations to become awkward and one-sided. No one enjoys that type of discussion!

Casual conversations and first encounters are a stumbling block for many of us. We fear that we will come across as unintelligent or boring. However, small talk is not supposed to be brilliant! It is the first step of communication. The person who casually comments on the upcoming hurricane season is not seeking a five-minute dissertation of scientific facts and figures. There is a place and time for lengthy discussions, but usually not within the first thirty seconds of meeting someone. Do not fear the exchange of short pleasantries or believe they are trivial.

No matter how long the conversation, a good listener realizes he never has to worry what to say next. As the other person speaks, we are given plenty of fodder for conversation if we listen carefully. Even discovering something as simple as where that person works will provide numerous options to pursue. How long have they worked for the company? Do they enjoy that line of work? What are their duties? The possibilities are endless.

Every answer gives us even more information, too. By focusing on the person's words, we receive many potential conversational paths to follow. This eliminates the panic we might feel if we are simply formulating our next sentence in our heads rather than listening. Don't worry what to say next- let the other individual provide the answer!

OVERCOMING

"Perhaps the most important skill we can all develop is listening. Everyone has something to say, but so few people listen that when you do it instantly makes you stand out. And if you're not sure what the other person's message is, it makes people feel good when you try to clarify. "Are you saying that...?" Nothing puts someone on your side faster than letting them know that you were paying attention to their words. Make them feel like their words matter, and they'll treat you like you matter."
- Austin S. Camacho, author of the Hannibal Jones Mysteries
www.ascamacho.com

OBSTACLES

In order for us to listen, the other person must open up his mouth and talk. Asking questions encourages his participation in the discussion. He may seem reluctant or slow to respond, but do not let this discourage the pursuit of meaningful dialogue. That person might be unaccustomed to the attention or even suspicious as to why anyone would find him interesting. Persist with a genuine, caring attitude and honest motive. You will eventually coax a detailed and engrossing response. And if you discover his hot button, prepare for the sleeper to awaken.

What is this mysterious 'hot button'? How do I find it? This may require a little detective work on your part. Sometimes it might be obvious, such as a sports team logo on their apparel. You may receive a little snippet of information regarding a new baby or recent accomplishment. If the opportunity allows it, discover a few facts about the person's family or hobbies before meeting in person. This attention to detail will make them feel important as well.

Often it will require a few probing questions to uncover a topic dear to their heart. Once you have located a hot button, the person will be more than willing to elaborate on the subject. You will receive enough information to supply you with questions all night long if neccessary. The other person will come alive with enthusiasm, and if it's an intense passion, they will transform right before your very eyes!

Not all questions are created alike, either. Open-ended questions elicit the best response and provide elaborate replies. If the person can answer with a simple yes, no or other one-word reply, then we can bet that is all they will offer! Ask questions that require an explanation rather than confirmation. Certainly, we do not want to sound like an interrogator, but it is difficult to engage in stimulating conversation when we receive no feedback. Eventually the discussion will become very one-sided and awkward.

All of these things tend to go against our very nature, though. We want to talk about ourselves! It is challenging at first to truly focus on another person's concerns, goals and opinions. Developing genuine and sincere interest will take time and practice. Yet, we must learn if we are to connect with those around us in a meaningful manner. Monopolizing a conversation just to satisfy our own desire to talk will not endear us to other people.

A poor conversationalist is like a five-year-old child. He comes at us wide open and eager, flitting from one high point of his life to another like a nervous moth in a lamp shop. He's so eager to tell us everything that we can hardly get a word in edgewise! Occasionally this person's boasts will sound arrogant, but usually he is just innocently rambling and completely unaware of his behavior.

While this trait is endearing and amusing in five-year-old, it does not suit us well as adults. Others will come to view us as shallow, insensitive, and uncaring. Unintentional or not, we drive people away with this selfish behavior. Resist the urge to control conversations in this manner, or you'll soon discover that no one lingers in your presence!

Encourage others to discuss their thoughts and feelings and speak only when invited to do so. If we approach others with a sincere and caring spirit, eager to known them as an individual person, their responses will truly amaze us. Our interest will fill their need for acceptance and approval, feeding their ego. They will walk away from these encounters feeling good about themselves- and us!

"That good listeners are rare is obvious. But here's a secret: if you listen well, people will think you're fascinating."
- Paula Berinstein, The Writing Show
www.writingshow.com

If we are to connect with those around us, we must hear each unique voice and expression of ideas. Listening is one behavior we can easily modify, and it will expand our horizons as we focus our attention elsewhere. And life becomes so much simpler when we no longer focus on ourselves!

In a nutshell...
- Listening requires effort and practice.
- Small talk is okay.
- Shift the focus to that person by asking questions.
- Practice open-ended questions and find a person's hot button.
- Resist the urge to sound like a five-year-old child.

12

Making Good Impressions

The animal that steps in mud will leave an impression of its foot as a physical reminder of his brief presence. In a similar manner, we leave impressions on those with whom we come in contact every day. Obviously, we hope that impression is good!

Of utmost importance is the very first impression. As the saying goes, you'll never have a second chance to make a good first impression. This is precisely why you should be prepared for personal encounters at all times. You may not have the luxury of a perfectly planned meeting every time, so presenting your best on a consistent basis should be one of your goals.

How are impressions formed? Memories come from events that strike an emotional chord, whether positive or negative, and impressions are formed in a similar fashion. Our view of others is shaped by verbal and non-verbal communication and by physical attributes. We receive and interpret these signals and compare them to past experiences. Our previous encounters carry much weight and guide our responses, decisions, and impressions.

People tend to dwell upon and recall negative far more often than positive. This is why poor first impressions are difficult to overcome. If you feel that you have caused someone to form a negative impression, then you must act quickly. As time passes, the negative imprint multiplies and compounds the problem. A second, more favorable impression, occurring soon after the first, will begin to reverse the damage. If an apology is in order, then do not hesitate to offer one. Take steps to correct the situation before it's too late to change the individual's assessment and over-all opinion.

Occasionally, you will make little or no impression at all. This occurs for a number of reasons. An incredibly brief encounter might not provide enough time to form a lasting memory. We pass hundreds of people each day, few of whom we will recall five minutes later. Sometimes the person you meet is too self-absorbed to notice anyone else. Focused on his own thoughts, he is oblivi-ous to the world. Most of the people we meet in our daily exist-ence will fall into one of those two categories.

However, sometimes the fault lies with us instead, and we simply fail to act or respond in a noticeable manner. This can become a real problem if your goal is to impress new clients or upper management. How can we hope to instill a favorable im-pression if they fail to remember us five minutes later? We must learn to stand out from the crowd- in a positive way, of course. No need to attract attention unless we are on our best behavior!

So how does one go about making a good impression? If a first impression is critical and poor one difficult to overcome, how do we ensure a pleasant recollection in the minds of those we en-counter? Let me outline a few simple rules you should follow:

- Offer a smile. Nothing conveys acceptance or friendliness quite like a genuine smile. It also reduces or eliminates your fear. You cannot smile and feel scared or worried at the same time!
- Maintain eye contact. This conveys respect for the person and belies a good self-image on your part.
- Use the other's name and often. You will convey courtesy and respect, not to mention remember the person's name by repeating it several times during the course of conversation.
- Focus on that person. As we discussed earlier, do not dominate the conversation, but rather allow the other person to become the center of attention.

As with all people skills, there are no gimmicks, but there is a secret when it comes to impressions. One surefire way to make a good impression on someone is to let him know he is making one on you! If you follow the basic rules during the encounter, he will regard your behavior as a vote of confidence. That person will conclude that you view him as important, valuable, and respectable. In his mind, he thinks, "Hey, he believes I'm really somebody!" Your consideration will in turn impress that person in a most meaningful manner.

"Leaders are active listeners first."
- Bill Myers, Columbus (OH) Health Commissioner,
1980-2002

One way to destroy a good impression is to disagree. By this, I'm not suggesting that you blindly agree with everything the other person says! We all possess the right to our own opinion. However, contradiction just for the sake of disagreeing is not permissible. You will only create bad feelings and a general sense of unease in the relationship. The worst-case scenario is the formation of an enemy.

Agreeing with others confirms their self-worth and feeds their ego. It implies that their opinions really do matter. Regardless of the subject or topic, we can usually offer a positive comment or verification of their beliefs. Use past experiences to demonstrate shared feelings. If someone mentions a common favorite vacation spot, then agree with his assessment. However, if our personal experience was less than enjoyable, then it is far wiser to remain silent on the matter then to slam that person's beliefs!

Sometimes ugly personality traits can interfere with creating good impressions. Maintaining standards is one thing, but implying excellence without fault is another. Resist the urge to portray yourself as perfect. According to my faith, there was only one perfect person that ever lived. The rest of us fall short of that lofty aspiration! If we attempt to sound perfect, it only comes across as phony and reeking of false pride. Placing ourselves of a pedestal guarantees only one thing- at some point, we will fall, and fall hard indeed.

Another killer of good impressions is endeavoring to one-up others in conversation. We only succeed in annoying the other person. As with portraying ourselves as perfect, our superiority will sound shallow and self-serving. When someone announces a personal accomplishment, do not respond by informing him of a similar or better achievement. That small triumph is important to the other person and our declaration of greater success might discourage and diminish his self-esteem. Allow that individual to enjoy his moment of glory. He will remember and appreciate our genuine congratulations.

It should now be apparent that creating a good impression depends heavily on our ability to make the other person feel good. We need to stroke his ego, not our own. Cockiness and self-assurance have no place in the scenario. This should come as a relief! We no longer feel pressured to present infallible perfection.

So, leave the superhero costume at home. Set forth with the goal of inspiring self-worth in others. Armed with this objective, you will master the art of creating good impressions.

In a nutshell...
- First impressions are difficult to change.
- People tend to dwell on the negative.
- Learn to make a GOOD impression.
- Let that person know he impresses you.
- Agreeing with a person feeds his ego.
- Do not one-up others or sound perfect.

13

Communication and Accessibility

Relationships do not grow and thrive by themselves. Contact in one form or another must occur. Even business relationships require proximity. This implies that people need to access and communicate with us on a fairly regular and consistent basis.

Communication is so vital that our way of life would not exist without it. Can you imagine the state of our highway system if ideas and plans were not shared? It would result in utter chaos! (Not to mention create a slew of unhappy drivers.) Every conception requires communication to come together and properly function, from a giant skyscraper to a monthly newsletter. Relationships are no different!

The saying that absence makes the heart grow fonder may sound incredibly romantic, but in real life, bonds slowly fade without contact. Separation does not encourage relationships to grow but instead causes them to wither and die. We require steady input to feel and remain connected. Most companies realize we need constant reminders, which is why we see the same commercial ten times during a thirty-minute TV show. That much contact is not necessary for all relationships to flourish, but we can clearly see how important it is to stay connected.

Communicating and spending time with another person helps us to get to know that individual. Relationships move through several stages in the progression as well, from the discussion of facts to the exchange of opinions to the sharing of feelings. Every step requires conversation at some level and a give and take from both individuals.

Long distance relationships are common in our society today, but at some point, physical contact is required for continued growth. Body language and mannerisms play a huge role in human interaction. Some things are only communicated through eye contact or a friendly handshake. The sharing of activities and accumulation of similar experiences adds to a friendship, providing yet another level of understanding. We crave physical nearness for these very reasons.

When we talk about relationships, we usually think of those with family and friends. However, connections should be developed in all areas of our life. Don't forget professional contacts. Build a connection to those with whom we do business as well. Nothing strengthens a working environment like the camaraderie of friendship. A close bond with our co-workers will strengthen our support system and provide trusted allies in times of need. Depending on our profession, such ties could one day save our life, too!

Do not limit work contacts to just those at our level, either. We should forge friendships with those who rank above and below us as well. Now, a supervisory position will limit the extent and depth of our personal relations with subordinates. However, we still need to connect with these people and let them know we are real. This improves our overall work environment, as subordinates will feel more at ease in our presence.

How do we develop these relationships? First and foremost, we must be accessible. The supervisor who hides in his office, venturing out only when he requires something, will feel no connection with his employees. We must make ourselves available to these people! Our followers want and need to share information, and relish the opportunity to speak with us directly. Never forget the position we hold in business, but do not fear connecting verbally and physically with subordinates on a personal level.

As we learned with listening and forging good impressions, our willingness to communicate and reach out to others will accomplish many things. We demonstrate appreciation as we develop business and personal relationships. People desire understanding, and since meanings can be lost in translation from one person to another, our willingness to seek the original source will satisfy this yearning. We appeal to the basic human need for approval and verification of importance. Our actions say 'I care'!

We also learn from others. A good leader circulates among the troops, expressing interest and asking questions. The input we receive from this direct contact is invaluable for making quality decisions. We may not actively participate in the daily grind of business, but the workers in the trenches can inform us of the actual situation. Our accessibility becomes a tremendous asset! After all, how can a leader make informed decisions if he has no idea what's happening?

Personal contact wins loyalty in all forms of relationships, whether business-connected or private. The husband who provides ample attention to his wife wins her loyalty just as a business partner is won over by professional consideration. That is why it is imperative that we apply this behavior to all situations and cultivate consistency. These skills will not be as effective if we simply turn them off and on at will! Sporadic behavior sends a negative message.

Learn to openly communicate with those around you, and place yourself in a position that invites association. Leave your comfort zone and reach out to people. If you remain in isolation, you'll discover your world is now an island- and it is a very long swim back to shore!

In a nutshell...
- Communication is a vital part of relationships.
- Physical contact strengthens friendships.
- Build both personal and business relationships.
- Be accessible.
- Reach out and understand other people.
- Communicate to learn and instill loyalty.

14

Maintaining Friendships

In our disposable society, we tend to forget that some things are well worth preserving. Friendships are perhaps the most precious commodity a man can possess. They are intangible but invaluable to our survival and well-being. At the end of our lives, friendships are the wealth that matters.

Often we define who we are and where we are going by our friendships. Human relations affect all areas- our careers, our families, our recreational activities. We cannot ignore the intricate web of relationships in our world nor underestimate their importance. True success and wealth is measured in the number of friends we possess. And the friend we make tomorrow just might change the course of our life!

Friendships wither and die for a number of reasons. Neglect is a common cause for a relationship's eventual demise. Sometimes this occurs early and while the friendship is still in the acquaintance phase. Two people may discover they share little common ground. There's just not enough present to spark further growth in the relationship.

Close friendships can dissolve as well. Lack of contact and maintenance, coupled with no shared experiences, can result in shriveling relationships. People grow apart and change, leaving behind one group in favor of a new circle of friends. Often we find we are on the giving end of a one-sided relationship and must decide whether to continue in our efforts. If a friendship turns destructive, it may need to be curtailed as well. The act of ending a relationship is never easy, regardless of the reason or cause.

Disagreements tend to be the leading cause of failed relationships. Our current divorce rate attests to the truth of that statement! A minor altercation escalates into a major fight, and before we realize what is happening, the friendship abruptly ends. Feuds can carry on for generations and all from one small disagreement of opinion.

Author C. Denise Sutton, (a friend who prodded me into the area of speaking & lecturing), has this to say about maintaining friendships despite our differences:

We all have different ways and reasons for forming friendships. As a person travels through life, he tends to cling to those who have similar beliefs. However, as this person matures, he begins to realize that no matter how close he is to someone, at one time or another, he will have some views that oppose those of his counterpart. A person who constantly pounces upon those who do not view things exactly as he does can easily offend those around him. However, a true leader must learn to be open-minded and realize that different opinions are a way of life. People's beliefs are affected by an array of factors including past experiences, teachings, and even something as simple as a pet peeve. In dealing with others, one must realize that a person's belief is built on years of repetitious enforcement and any challenge to that belief or way of thinking is not only an insult to that person's way of thinking, but to their core character. One way to lose a person quickly and put them on the defensive is to blatantly criticize their belief without showing any indication that you have made any attempt to see the situation from their perspective.

Never give another person the impression that you are trying to automatically change their point of view just because it does not coincide with yours. Tact is the key for keeping the lines of communication open and one should counteract differing views, if possible, with either a supporting fact, law, or policy, and in a manner that is neither "pushy" or aggressive. Once a person decides to express their disagreement with or correction on an issue, the blow to the other person can be cushioned in two ways: 1) Express to the other person that you understand how or why they think or feel the way they do, and 2) Explain the rationale for why you feel the way you do instead. A person may disagree with you at first, but change their opinion, after looking at your feedback.

Always remember, too, in any process, that you both can be either right or wrong. One must learn to pick which battles justify being fought. If you differ from someone on the type of mate you would choose, for instance, then realize that we all are unique and that it is ok that the qualities important to someone else do not matter to you. An exception would be if the characteristics that you differ on are character flaws that could be life altering, i.e. the person you would choose has a history of murdering others or swindling them out of their life savings. Remember, also, when differing with someone, you want to stay on the same wavelength as the other person, by stressing that although you may differ on an issue, it is minor compared to the issues that you agree with. This is a way to remind others that regardless of your differences, you are on the "same page" when it comes to important issues. Remember a difference of opinions does not have to affect a friendship but often gives a person all the more reason to have a friend that, instead of seeing things the same way, helps them to grow by giving them a different perspective on situations.

Another point to make is to be sure that you are not "arguing" with someone whom you actually agree with. This is where listening skills come in that are effective enough to catch the whole message of what is being said before a response is given. Always be generous with praise before and after criticizing someone and only give the criticism if it is absolutely needed to accomplish a task or if the person himself asks for the feedback.

- *Author C. Denise Sutton, www.mywordsandme.com*

Pick and choose battles very carefully! Refuse to fight with a fighter, especially one who derives sheer joy from arguing. That person is not worth the headache and ill feelings that will result. Remember that arguing does not win the argument. It only adds to negative feelings and reduces self-esteem. If we feel we've won the argument, we've probably just lost the war- and a good friend to boot!

Unless it involves moral or ethical issues, it is not worth hurting the relationship over a minor difference of opinion. When disagreements arise, we always have the option of compromise. Disagree with someone only if it is absolutely necessary. If someone dials 911 and gives the wrong address, that's a good time to step in and correct the error. However, if your friend misquotes a football game's statistics, will it really matter in the grand scheme of life? Is it really worth chipping at their self-image just to set the facts straight?

The secret to maintaining friendships is effort. We must make emotional effort and sacrifices, as well as physical acts of reaching out to others, to ensure our relationships run smooth. Failure to do these simple things leads to a very lonely existence indeed!

Now, which of your friends deserves a call or visit today?

In a nutshell...
- Human relations affect all areas of our lives.
- Avoid the friendship-killers.
- Learn to see things from all perspectives
- Accept the differences in people.
- Do not disagree unless absolutely necessary.

15

Generous With Praise

If we want to make a valuable deposit in another person, offering a genuine and sincere compliment is a priceless act. By praising another's actions, words, or person, it affirms his value and worth. It satisfies that insatiable need for approval we all possess.

The effects of praise are easily viewed in a child's reaction. Tell junior his drawing is beautiful and he will positively glow with joy! Compliment his ability to maintain a clean room, and he will feel inspired to continue this behavior. To a child, these affirmations are like applause and cheers. You have noticed his efforts and rewarded him with praise and a proverbial cookie. (Sometimes he receives a real cookie, too!)

The need for this type of positive reinforcement does not diminish as we age. The small child, still desperate for approval, continues to reside within each person. Unfortunately, the amount of praise we receive dwindles as we enter adulthood. This means we cherish even more the smatterings of genuine commendations when they do occur.

Praise is a special gift. The more we give, the more we receive. The recipient of the acclamation experiences joy and satisfaction, and so does the giver. Once we fully appreciate the positive reactions on both sides of the coin, we are more motivated to commend others. We are apt to seek out opportunities to offer praise and encouragement, because we will feel good, too.

We may be stingy with our money, but throw restraint out the window when it comes to praise! It is not a limited commodity. We possess an infinite amount of affirmations and will only lose the ability to produce more if we fail to give them away. The more we shower others with compliments and gratitude, the greater our capacity grows. Hoarding praise only results in diminishing results, as those who offer compliments infrequently are also the least likely to receive such glory.

Before preceding any further, perhaps some examples of praise-worthy situations are in order. After all, there are more opportunities than simply congratulating a friend when he receives a promotion at work. Moments of great triumph deserve acclamations, but the need for praise extends beyond major accomplishments. Many small occurrences in day to day living garner the need for our attention.

Consider the following scenarios:

- The wife who is prompt with dinner preparations
- The store clerk who is friendly and helpful
- The postal worker who brings our mail to the door so it will not be crushed in the mailbox
- The child who picks up his toys without being asked

As you can see from these situations, praise is also gratitude! It can be as simple as offering a sincere thank you. Many of us have forgotten this common courtesy or offer it without thinking. We take for granted the efforts of other people, whether they occupy a retail position or reside within our own family.

The challenge is to seek opportunities to say thank you. Take note of those providing a service and express gratitude. Even if the act is performed with a negative attitude, offer a sincere word of thanks. Our appreciation may transform that individual's entire day and change how they deal with the next person. It is the unexpected expressions of gratefulness that carry the most weight.

Compliments also fall within the realm of praise. Informing a woman that we like her new hairstyle or a man that his sports coat is incredibly sharp are examples of effective compliments. Our words affirm their personal tastes and boost their self-images. Complimenting others is a habit of choice. Every individual possesses some quality on which we can offer a kind word. If you doubt this proclamation, then try increasing your powers of observation and see what happens!

Why so much emphasis on praise? It feeds our basic human need for approval and demonstrates recognition. When we compliment others, it exhibits our belief that they are important. Relationships flourish and grow under the influence of gratitude and acclimation, even in the workplace. Praise lets our subordinates and co-workers know that we value their opinion. This encourages the exchange of information and ideas.

As leaders, we must perfect the art of extolling others. Our followers will respond favorably and perform better when they realize their actions receive attention. However, we need to notice more than just their accomplishments. Reward their efforts as well as results. Our subordinates may not succeed in every endeavor but should not feel afraid to try. Praise for their efforts removes the fear of failure when they attempt something new. After all, companies need employees who embrace innovation if they hope to move forward in business!

Praise also softens the blow of criticism. When we know we've failed, it helps if we are told we are successful in other areas. Situations will arise that require us to offer constructive criticism. Sandwich those words in between positive encouragement. (Praise- criticism- praise.) Criticism without the compliment inspires no one! Master the sandwich approach in all areas of life.

The habit of gratitude and praise also provides a unique benefit, because there is one person we cannot applaud- ourselves! If we are actively commending others, they will respond in a similar fashion and return our compliments. Another person's affirmation will most certainly carry more weight. The truth of the matter is that we simply cannot endorse ourselves. It is one thing to mention a recent accomplishment, but to proudly congratulate our actions in the presence of others will reek of false pride!

As you can see, offering praise and affirmation is vital when dealing with other people. Our words feed their hunger for approval and inspire the continuation of achievement. Since we will reap benefits as well, do not act the miser. Be generous with praise!

In a nutshell...
- We all crave praise and acceptance.
- Give praise and affirmation freely.
- Remember to show gratitude.
- Seek ways to compliment others.
- Praise efforts as well as accomplishments.
- Those who offer praise will also receive it.

16

Motivating Others

Wouldn't it be incredible if we could just wave a magic wand and people would do what we want them to do? If only it was that simple! It requires effort and finesse, not to mention a certain amount of patience. Fortunately, motivating others is a skill that can be mastered with practice.

The best place to begin and one of the easiest ways to motivate others is by example. Of course, this implies that we set a good example! Human nature dictates that people will adopt all of our bad attributes and only a portion of our good habits. The trick is to exhibit as few bad habits as is possible. Remember the expression 'Do as I say, not as I do' holds little weight here, because people imitate our actions faster than our words.

OVERCOMING

"Leadership is serving by example. In the Western culture, success is measured by how many people serve you. True leadership is measured by how many people you serve!"
- Bill Wilson, author & Pastor of The Lord's Table

There are several methods we can employ to set a good example. As previously stated, action speaks louder than words. Therefore, set out to be the hardest worker in the group or organization. Most people simply seek guidance and will hit the ground running behind a leader. Once they observe our behavior, they duplicate our efforts. Even those less motivated will feel prompted by a sense of guilt! Regardless of the reason for spurred action, other people will work harder when we set the example of proper work habits.

Our interactions with others also provide a shining example. If we are polite and friendly, treating every person with respect, those around us will take notice. In this day and age, any display of manners will draw attention! Our proficiency at handling situations and encounters will set the example for those watching, and they will slowly adopt some of these good habits and traits. Not all individuals will change, but our behavior will affect many.

A perfect example of how behavior can be altered lies in one of my previous places of employment. Cursing was a major problem for many of the employees at this company. Since most of these words were not a part of my vocabulary, I made a conscious decision to refrain from uttering any phrase that sounded negative or defamatory. Within a couple weeks, and without a single word of complaint from me, all of the cursing in my presence ceased. My example made a difference!

Sometimes, in order to motivate others, we must first discover what they want. Since human nature dictates we tend to consider our own needs before those of others, we need to tap into this desire and use its power. If we understand a man's true goal, and it aligns with our ambitions, demonstrating how he can achieve these aspirations will assure that both parties win. When he sees how he will benefit, our recommendations and directions will not fall upon deaf ears, and he will feel motivated to pursue a common goal.

If we really want to light a fire, asking for ideas and suggestions sparks a blaze. People will give total physical effort if they feel they are giving some of their brainpower as well. Encourage creativity and accept advice from others so they will not feel as if we are only interested in their brawn. Occasionally, their proposals will be exactly what we had in mind all along. If our followers feel the suggestions and ideas are all their own, they will pursue the goal with added determination and confidence! We cannot ask for a more powerful ally than a man motivated by his own dreams.

As we often discover, people respond to persuasion. Suggestions, rather than direct orders or coercion, will prompt favorable reactions. Yes, order is required in the workplace. When no one follows directions, chaos reigns. However, one person barking orders makes for a miserable work environment. When people feel as if they lack the ability to offer input and have no control, morale slips and purpose is lost in the daily grind. Asking for compliance with rules and suggesting the proper procedure yields far better results. It encourages a more positive environment as well.

The pyramids were likely built by slaves who knew nothing of the wonders they were creating. However, that slave driver mentality does not translate well to present day! We prefer to understand the cause behind our labor. Sharing the vision will allow others to feel connected to the project and the goal. Let those assisting us know where they stand in terms of progress. If they can see the light at the end of the tunnel, and the prize awaiting the completion of their task, they will continue to move forward.

"Successful leaders are life-long learners and they create 'learning organizations' that foster creativity and a commitment to work collectively to achieve the organization's vision."
- Bill Myers, Columbus (OH) Health Commissioner, 1980-2002

How many times has an encouraging word caused us to try harder? While working toward a goal, do not forget to offer verbal encouragement to those traveling the path with us. As we learned with praise, positive affirmation motivates people to new heights and causes them to stretch. They need to know when they are on the right track, too. Offer positive feedback as duties are performed and completed. This will ensure a duplication of those efforts and keep the organization running smooth.

Another creative means by which to motivate others is to master the art of storytelling. In the Bible, Jesus encouraged and instructed his followers through parables. Use this same form of motivation to inspire people. Look for historical or true-life stories similar in spirit or possessing parallel ambitions. By relating these stories to those struggling toward a goal, we demonstrate that it can indeed be attained. The knowledge that some-one else has successfully accomplished a task or reached the mark is a real confidence builder. Nothing motivates like a victorious testimony to the human spirit.

We might discover we need to employ a little friendly competition. Many people possess a strong drive to win. Throw down a challenge and just watch how it spurs others to action! This often results in increased productivity and fresh ideas. Of course, rivalry tactics should be used sparingly. There are those who fear intense competition or feel discouraged by contests. We may find half of our work force has given up if we set the stakes too high. And, if the battle to win becomes too fierce, an unpleasant and bitter war may develop! Do not place such emphasis on competition that people turn on one another. Keep it light and fun for all.

There are many ways to motivate. We might need to try several options to discover the one that works best in a given situation. Everyone responds to at least one form of motivation, though. Our job is to find the right match and stick with it!

In a nutshell...
- Motivate by setting a good example.
- Discover the desires of others.
- Allow others to contribute ideas.
- People respond to gentle persuasion.
- Encourage others and master storytelling.
- Employ friendly competition.

17

Refuse to Fight With a Fighter

Verbal battles are difficult to predict. One thing is certain, though. There is rarely a definite winner. Like a game of tic-tac-toe, intense disagreements often end in a draw with neither side willing to concede. The trick is not to learn how to win but to avoid these fights altogether.

How many times have you encountered a person who seems to relish a fight? He appears to derive great pleasure in pitting his wits against yours and will debate an issue for hours. If you've ever found yourself trapped in a discussion with one of these individuals, then you know there is little you can say to sway his opinion. In fact, the more opposition you display, the more determined that person becomes to counter your words. You simply cannot hope to win the argument.

When dealing with people of this nature, the safest course of action is to resist the urge to argue. If we do not fight back or grow defensive, we will remove the fun from their cat and mouse game. They will quickly lose interest and cease in their efforts to force a rise out of us. Refusing to fight is the only way we'll ever win this type of battle.

Fortunately, most people are not born fighters. Humans do possess an incredible stubborn streak, though. Right or wrong, we tend to stand by our beliefs and convictions. Compound this issue with a low self-image and defending our point of view becomes a matter of life or death!

It is this very self-survival instinct that causes a man to dig in his heels and refuse to budge. By challenging his opinion or conviction, we have by default attacked his ego. Since we crave approval and acceptance, this dismissal of his beliefs demonstrates disapproval and damages his self-esteem. Threatening another's self-image causes the defenses to rise and guarantees a fight to the bitter end. Defending his ego becomes more important than the issue itself.

Perhaps now it is apparent why winning quarrels is a lost cause from the beginning. People are simply not convinced by an argument. No amount of logic will change their minds. Drawing emotions into the foray only causes the situation to worsen. We might as well beat our heads against a brick wall! It is unlikely a resolution will be reached without injured feelings, and both parties will depart with a sense of unease.

Sometimes the results are even more devastating. Disagreements can escalate into full-scale wars where nothing is sacred. Attacks turn personal and eventually the original cause of the fight is lost in the confusion. Many friendships are dissolved under this type of pressure. Entire families can be torn apart by such feuds. The negative atmosphere and resulting feelings can even cause illness. There is simply no benefit to an eternal quarrel.

Ill feelings can linger long after the argument ends. If we do not let go of this anger, resentment will build. We will develop all manner of negative thoughts and feelings toward our perceived opposition. This only harms us and not our intended target, though. We may resort to other tactics. Thoughts of revenge may creep into our minds. At that point, we might even form a plan to get back at those who caused us personal injury.

Unfortunately, acting out of vengeance never yields positive results. It also blinds us to all else in life! We lose sight of goals and focus solely on our path of destruction. We can become so consumed with destroying an enemy that we lose as well in the process. Do not let this become your fate! If harboring grudges is a personal struggle for you, seek alternate means by which to release your frustration. If you did not win the argument, then you will certainly not win the war by focusing negatively on that person. Forgive, forget, and move on with life.

Since we can't win by arguing, we must try a soft approach instead. Rather than go to guns, discover exactly why that person feels so strongly about their opinion. Sometimes just the opportunity for a little understanding will satisfy his needs. By listening to his view or grief, we have the chance to diffuse the situation before it escalates into a quarrel. We might even discover that person has a valid point and choose to adopt the suggestion. Compromise does not imply cowardice or weakness, but rather the strength to admit we were wrong while possessing enough wisdom to see a better way.

Not all contention starts with us, though. (And if they do, perhaps it's time for a little self-analysis!) Disagreements can originate from within a group instead. We may find our friends quarreling or our subordinates exchanging less than positive words. A wise leader must move quickly to resolve tensions. If we allow anger and resentment to smolder, it will boil over at some point. This almost guarantees a halt in all forward progress.

Provide an outlet for negative feelings and grievances. Encourage others to work out their differences. You'll need to call upon your creative powers, but find a manner in which differences can be resolved. Weekly meetings where all can speak freely, private conferences involving the guilty parties, locking everyone in a room- whatever it takes to restore peace! If you can induce conversation and control the tone, the warring parties will usually come to an agreement. Often you will discover that it was simply a misunderstanding or falsely perceived insult that started the whole situation.

If quarrels always appear to arise around one particular individual, then evaluate the situation carefully. If that person is key to our success or a major contributor to the project, it may force us to tolerate and accept the troublesome behavior. However, if he is the proverbial crab in the bucket and qualifies only as a distraction, we may need to make an executive decision. Some people are simply more trouble than they are worth!

Arguments will occur despite the best of intentions and most well laid plans. The ability to diffuse the situation quickly is the quality of a great leader and distinguishes you from the pack. Take the high road and refuse to fight with the fighters. The simple act of living is enough of struggle!

In a nutshell...
- Do not fight with a fighter.
- Challenging another's beliefs attacks his ego.
- People are not convinced by an argument.
- Avoid resentment and acting out of vengeance.
- Use the soft approach to disagreements.
- Provide others an outlet for their grievances.

Key 3

Raising Self-Esteem

Our self-esteem is basically how we view ourselves. This private opinion affects everything from our relationships to our accomplishments. It controls our confidence or lack thereof. We are either set free or held hostage by our self-image.

We can never grow beyond our self-esteem's level. If we are to achieve more and live life fully, we must raise this personal opinion.

Which leads us to the third Key- raising self-esteem!

18

Self-Image Facts and Importance

Our self-esteem is the deciding factor in whether we succeed or fail in life. It is an intangible possession of incredible power. What exactly is this internal force and what shapes its attributes?

Self-esteem can be described as a sense of personal worth. It is self-respect, confidence, and genuine joy on the positive side and self-doubt, worthlessness, and unhappiness on the negative side. Our ability to handle situations and accomplish goals is determined by the amount of self-esteem we possess. At any given time, this can also fluctuate between sufficient amounts or serious deficiency.

To measure self-esteem, think of a ruler. Each of us possess an internal scale with zero in the middle and plus or minus on either side. Our feelings of personal value can be measured by where they fall on that scale. The average person fluctuates somewhere near zero or higher, feeling confident under certain circumstances and full of doubt at other moments. The higher we reside on the positive end of the ruler, the less often uncertainty and feelings of inadequacy creep into our minds.

Our self-image begins to develop when we are very young. Since we are born with a clean slate and no preconceived notions, self-esteem takes shape as we receive input from our surroundings. Sights, sounds, and the verbal tone of those with whom we have contact imprint our minds. Words become a strong influence as we learn to grasp language. We perceive our personal value based on these contributing factors.

When we grow old enough to act and think for ourselves, we contribute to the cultivation of our self-esteem as well. Based on previous input, our actions and words continue to mold our feelings of worth. We confirm or deny previous assessments of our merit as our experiences expand and multiply. Once we are adults, we should no longer rely on outside appraisal. Our self-image now becomes our sole responsibility.

Under ideal conditions, parents lay a solid foundation on which to build a great self-image. They encourage their children in every endeavor; praising accomplishments as well as efforts and lifting spirits when the results are less than successful. The entire family believes the children are capable and worthy. Friends, teachers, and others in positions of influence reinforce this message. In a perfect world, children reach adulthood with healthy self-images as a result of this positive input.

However, if that does not describe your upbringing, then join the club! Very few of us enjoyed such a positive and uplifting atmosphere.

On the contrary, we heard affirming words rather infrequently. The average child hears the word "no" around 200,000 times, and the word "yes" less than a fifth of that total. Since most people possess an average self-image, our parents were probably no different. They did not know how to build or lift ours any higher. Our friends probably did not offer any substantial contributions in that department, either. For most of us, possessing high or positive self-esteem was not a reality as a child, and we were more likely to attain a sense of worth after reaching adulthood.

What are the components of a negative self-image and how does it form? At its most basic, it develops from disaffirming re-inforcements and constant failure coupled with the refusal to continue. When we experience defeat and do not persist in our attempts, our self-esteem takes a blow. Couple that scenario with negative comments or rebuttals and results that are disastrous, and personal worth really plummets to the bottom. Confidences slips and fear of repeating the experience prevents us from trying again. This places our self-image on the negative side of the scale. The more often this occurs, and the cycle of negative reinforcement and failure is duplicated, the further self-esteem slips.

Human nature dictates that we are our own worst critic. Despite the critics surrounding us, we berate ourselves far more often and more effectively. We see the failings no one else witnesses and experience these shortcomings more intimately. Every mistake is amplified in our minds. This compounds negative self-esteem even further.

Much to our dismay, a negative self-image is evident in our actions and words, too. We make attempts to hide of true sense of worth with shaky results at best. Some people are angered by their sense of low personal value and lash out at the world. Their words are hurtful and full of resentment. They exhibit destructive behaviors and make poor choices in life. These attempts to justify one's personal value only pushes the self-image further into the negative. On the other side of the coin, some people will feel depressed by their lack of importance. This lack of confidence causes them to withdraw from society in some fashion. Their insecurities lead to shyness and reluctance to try new things. Either response is nothing more than a wall of defense. These people fear the discovery of their failures and go to great lengths to protect whatever ounce of self-esteem remains.

People accept us at our own self-appraisal. Poor self-esteem projects a negative image and others sense this low, personal assessment. Those we encounter accept this unspoken judgment as fact and may in turn contribute to this misconception. With a self-image already suffering, these negative reinforcements only confirm our personal assessments of unworthiness. As adults, we should no longer rely on outside influence to determine our worth. Unfortunately, we tend to allow the opinions of others add to our feelings of inferiority.

A good self-image is critical to long-term success. If we are to live a life filled with joy, achievement, and a sense of worth, we must cultivate a positive image of ourselves. Even if our lives were overwhelmed with negative contributions, we can raise our self-esteem. Once we recognize this fact and acknowledge the need and desire for improvement, we can begin to make the necessary changes.

Beginning is half the battle. If your self-esteem resides in the negative, only you can make the decision to change that fact. Once you have opted to modify your self-image, you are ready to take the next step and start leading a life enriched with personal value, fulfillment, and genuine joy.

In a nutshell...
- Self-esteem is a sense of personal worth
- One's self-image is either positive or negative on the scale
- Development begins when we are children
- Failure and negative reinforcement result in a poor self-image
- Our actions and words betray our personal opinion
- Positive self-esteem is crucial for success

19

Stop the Downward Spiral

The descent into a negative self-image is like a downward spiral, pulling us down the drain and into oblivion. This destructive process needs to cease before we can work on raising our self-esteem. We must let go of sabotaging habits, release guilt, and reprogram our beliefs if we are to climb out of the hole.

Author Darlene Ford Wofford shares with us this turning point in her life:

"What goes up must come down" is the scientific fact of gravity as stated by Sir Isaac Newton more than three centuries ago. Unfortunately, the opposite does not apply, except with the elevator or a bouncing rubber ball. Once drawn into a downward direction, the spiral continues until reaching bottom. Nevertheless, the downward spiral can be stopped and even reversed. Example: To bring a plane out of a tailspin the pilot pulls back on the throttle—redirecting the nose upward and utilizing air currents to its advantage—thus pulling it out of a fatal nose-dive to the ground. However, if the pilot doesn't maintain composure to assess the problem, and tap into the know-how to reverse the doomed course of crashing, all aboard sadly become victims of the ultimate downward spiral. If that pilot panicked, sense of command giving way to concentrating on the dreaded outcome, final destination of the hard, cold ground would be unavoidable. So it is with our attitude, energy, & outlook on life in general.

Case in point: Our mind is the determining factor and driving force of our destiny. What we focus on is what we inevitably get.

Without doubt, we are who and what we say and think we are. There are those who think and say "Without bad luck I wouldn't have any luck at all," or "I'm always broke—I can't get ahead," or "I'm always sick," or "I can't find the right person to love." They've "bought into" these thoughts such that their total existence is defined by them. Unfortunately, the more they think or say they're "unlucky" in love, health, money, and life in general, the more "unlucky" they become, and ultimately depression sets in from the stress of it all. Medical studies reveal that stress is one of the leading contributors to health issues such as heart attacks, diabetes, nervous disorders, obesity, and countless other illnesses in today's world of hectic, fast-paced schedules. Every other commercial on television or in magazines provides a "cure" or relief from these conditions, targeting those who suffer from them, (or who may convince themselves they do after seeing the ad).

Viewers respond by running to their doctors for the miracle "quick fix" as seen on TV. Doctors diagnose their patients as depressed, or suffering from stress and anxiety disorders, thus prescribing medicine. Pharmaceutical companies are thriving from the multiplicity of these medications designed for the treatment of stress and anxiety, yet these issues grow more prevalent within our society with each generation.

The more we think we're stressed, the more stressed we become. The more we say we're depressed, the more depressed we become. I speak from personal experience. It was the first Sunday afternoon of 2008 when I slipped on the wet bathroom floor, sending my feet out from under me as I landed flat and hard on my "south side where the sun doesn't shine." My husband and I feared the worst as I was unable to stand, until after what seemed like forever, and I later crawled to the bed where I remained the next few days. I refused the idea of going to the hospital for care— I was simply in too much pain. In fact, the more I declared I was in pain, the more intense my pain became. As I lay there suffering I assessed my situation as hopeless, thinking I would never be able to walk "normally" again. Doom and gloom filled my thoughts as I slipped further into the downward spiral state of "poor, poor, pitiful me." Depression, stress, anxiety and helplessness defined my existence, while my foremost thought was, "Why do things always happen to me?"

By Tuesday morning with no real sign of improvement, my stress intensified knowing I was scheduled to present a "motivational" speech that upcoming Saturday—only four days away! I *almost* convinced myself that my husband was right in his recommendation I should call to cancel the event. The operative word here is "almost." As a woman of integrity, I'm always intent on fulfilling my promises and doing what I say I will do when I say I will do it. I couldn't picture making that call to cancel such an important event.

It was time to weigh my options, make a decision and take action. I had two options: Cancel my engagement or snap out of it and feel better. The first option was unacceptable and the second option was unlikely, short of a miracle.

I struggled to get out of bed and while making my way to the bathroom—all crouched over like an old crone—I caught my reflection in the full-length mirror. There it was, the disturbingly pitiful image of myself all bent over with the grimace of pain on my face. That was not an attractive look for me—or anyone else, for that matter. I sighed, but then chuckled at the unsightly mess I had become and declared with no uncertainty that I would pull myself out of this situation. The question was "How?"

I've taught others through the years how to stop and even reverse the destructible Downward Spiral by developing the "Attitude of Gratitude." It was high time I practiced what I preached—I had to pull back on my mind's "throttle" to pull me up and out of the tailspin into which I had fallen. The only way to do that is to replace the negative thoughts with positive ones—instead of dwelling on what's WRONG in my life, concentrate on what's RIGHT and the things for which I am thankful.

I shuffled over to my desk for a pad of paper and a pen. Exhausted and groaning in dire pain, I crawled back into bed intent on thinking of just three things for which I was grateful, and writing them down. Of course, my husband and two sons came to mind, my sister, my brother, my family, my friends, my home, etc. I couldn't stop with three, but continued down the page and onto a second and a third. Then the most amazing thing happened. Before I realized it I was no longer lying flat on my back, but had slid up onto the pillow and into a sitting position. It was

WORKING! I was stopping the destructible downward spiral dead in its tracks! By the next day the pain had subsided such that I went to the doctor to be examined. Although my hip was deeply bruised, x-rays confirmed no permanent damage had resulted from my fall. By Saturday I was walking upright like a healthy human being, without the slightest grimace of pain on my face, and no one was the wiser to my painful experience.

Every night before going to sleep I have developed the habit of recording three good things that happened that day or three things for which I am thankful. I keep it next to my bed so I can read over it first thing in the morning. It's incredible how it affects my days when I begin with positive thoughts, while anticipating what good things I will be writing about that evening. I look forward to each day and what it holds in store for me, as I remain conscious of my Attitude of Gratitude and remember: The more I say or think I'm blessed, the more reasons for which to feel blessed appear in my life!

The following is the wonderful exercise I use in developing and maintaining my "Attitude of Gratitude." It worked so well for me after my fall, I have continued the practice and highly recommend it to others. Try it out for just seven consecutive days, and after you see the difference in your outlook on life, you will want to continue as I have. This is one habit you won't want to break! (Required materials for this exercise: Paper and a pen/pencil).

I AM WHAT I THINK AND SAY I AM!

Choose the adjective/s that best describe how you desire to be in life: Successful, Motivated, Grateful, Spiritual, Inspired, Loving, Healthy, Happy, Generous, Financially Independent, Wealthy, Determined, etc.

The more *(Successful) I THINK I AM, the more *(Successful) I BECOME!

The more*(Motivated) I SAY I AM, the more *(Motivated) I BECOME!

Complete the following just before you go to sleep & review them first thing in the morning:

Down the left side of the page list the 7 days of the week, leaving spaces to write three good things that happened that day, and/or three things for which you are thankful. (See the following example):

Monday
Today I'm thankful because...
1. I enjoy a loving marriage.
2. I met my project's deadline.
3. I arrived at work and returned home safely.
   Fill Your Nights with Dreams of Discovery...
   Fulfill Your Days With the Fascinations of Exploring.
   - Darlene Ford Wofford—January, 1984
   ©The Spirited Southerner www.SpiritedSoutherner.com

To change who we are, we must change our thinking. Let go of the negative and painful weight that contributes to a poor self-image. Decide right now that it's time for a change. Only then will the downward spiral cease, allowing us to begin building positive self-esteem.

In a nutshell...
- We must act to reverse the downward spiral
- The negative in our mind compounds the problem
- We can control this spiral by making a decision
- Recall the good and positive of life
- Refuse to continue down the spiral

20

Take Mental Charge

Between our ears lies the most intellectual, resourceful, and powerful force on earth. Our brains have the capacity to make split-second decisions and remain focused on a particular course of action. We cannot allow this incredible resource to remain idle. If we expect to raise our self-esteem and accomplish our goals, we must put our minds to work.

If the self-image is to improve then responsibility must be accepted. We cannot continue to blame past circumstances and situations. Once we reach adulthood, we forfeit the right to play the victim card. Regardless of yesterday's events, we are now in charge of the present. There are great tragedies in life, but nothing is more pathetic than a person needlessly paralyzed by their own perceived injustices. We cannot change the past, but we can assume responsibility for our future.

One of the first items we need to control is our internal voice. The chatterbox in our heads is detrimental to our self-esteem as well as our attitude. Develop awareness of the words uttered silently in the mind. Are the phrases uplifting or downgrading? Remove belittling words of condemnation from your vocabulary. Even if no one around offers an encouraging word, play the role of cheerleader for yourself. Allow your stream of conscious to inspire and uplift. Do not speak as if you are your own worst enemy!

What about external negative forces? After all, our minds do not receive condemnation just from our internal voice. We communicate a low self-image to our consciousness by other means as well. Feeling a lack of confidence in our physical appearance, we'll purposefully select the least flattering clothes to wear. In the company of someone we admire or desire to know better, we'll act inappropriately just to prove they will not like us. Such behavior is counter-productive. If we want to feel valuable as a person, we must act and speak the part of a worthy individual.

Our voice and behavior are probably not the only items in need of modification. Every day of our lives, we are barraged with negative sounds, images, and stimuli. From the daily news to negative co-workers, we are assaulted on all sides. Many aspects of our society are negative and it can prove difficult to avoid the onslaught. However, there are certain things we can control, either by replacing negative with positive input or completely eliminating the source.

The aspects of your life requiring change depend on your current habits and overall need for growth. You might be better served stopping at the gym rather than the bar after work. If your current reading list focuses solely on 'celebrity' magazines, try devouring a self-help book every week instead. Altering your evening hours so there is less network television will allow more time for working on projects with your kids or taking a walk with your spouse. These are just a few suggestions, but they provide a general idea of changes to implement.

It is vital that you monitor what enters your brain. Give your mind something constructive on which to focus. Feed it with new information and positive thoughts so that it might grow and develop. Negative and minimal input tends to stagnate the brain. Shower your mind with challenging and stimulating thoughts and ideas. Plan a trip to your local library. Take up a new and exciting hobby. Expand your horizons! In order to achieve a higher self-image, your mind needs to stretch as well.

Do not forget to feed your physical body, either. Focus on healthy choices for your life. Exercise invigorates both body and mind, and it's a great way to deal with stress. As your physical conditions improve, so will your self-esteem. You will feel energized and refreshed.

It may appear as if there's a lot of negative to eliminate! If unsure of where to begin, create a list of desired changes. From this list, decide what can be done to improve life and how to achieve this goal. Sweeping changes work for some people, especially when accompanied by an emotionally charged, life-changing event, but most of us fare better taking small steps. Tackle one or two items every week until the end of the list is reached. Do not waver from these decisions and remember that a relapse is not a complete failure. Break out of the negative surrender pattern and simply try again.

OVERCOMING

Recognize that making the effort is in itself a success. Decide what steps will lead to achieving your goals and accept that taking those steps makes you a winner every day, long before the goal is achieved. If you want to lose weight, don't fret the number on the scales. But you should feel good at the end of every day you stick to your diet, and at the end of every workout, or whatever strategy you've chosen. Each time you have a small success, feel proud of yourself because you know you will eventually reach the ultimate goal.
- Austin S. Camacho, author of the Hannibal Jones Mysteries
www.ascamacho.com

 OBSTACLES

Another exercise that will help maintain focus involves creating two lists. On one sheet of paper, write down every positive attribute. List the tasks you perform well; what skills and strengths you possess; what tangibles reside in your life; etc. Write down everything! On the other sheet, list the negative. When you have completed both lists, read through them one more time and then proceed to tear up the list of negative attributes. Shred it to bits! Not only is the act of destroying this list liberating, it also leaves you with just one list on which to focus. Now you possess a starting point from which to build your self-image.

Self-esteem is all about how we view ourselves. If we don't like what we see, how can we possibly like ourselves? We hear 'accept yourself', but what we really need to accept and embrace is our incredible potential. We CAN turn around a poor self-image and develop a sense of personal worth and value. As our self-esteem rises, so will feelings of genuine self-love, confidence, self-respect, and happiness. Armed with renewed worth as a human being, we'll be able to face that person in the mirror!

Raising our level of self-esteem requires taking charge of our world- our thoughts, our actions, and the types of stimuli that occupy our time. No one else can make these decisions for us. We must step up and reclaim our lives!

In a nutshell...
- Take charge of your inner voice
- Control your behaviors and actions
- Eliminate external negative stimuli
- Feed your mind and body
- Take steps to implement changes
- Embrace your potential

21

Discipline a Success Image

Cultivating a success image involves more than just altering one's attire. In order to truly dress for success, we must begin with the inside. Genuine traits of leadership and prosperity cannot be faked, regardless of the outer parcel design. A successful person is a complete package.

We must dress for the occasion, of course. First impressions and perceptions are critical. We should always present ourselves as professional, regardless of our vocation or expertise. If there is a dress code in place, select attire that is equivalent to or higher than that standard. Even if our job only requires t-shirts and jeans due to heavy work, we can still wear fresh, untattered jeans and clean, appropriate t-shirts. Try to dress one notch higher when venturing casually into public as well. Not only will we look better, we will feel better, too!

There is one quality all victorious leaders possess- charisma! It's the trait that gives certain people a magnetic personality. Those in the presence of such magnetism are drawn to that individual. It is not important for those exhibiting charisma to possess the greatest intelligence or beauty, either. They simply enjoy a special ability to attract others as if charmed by a spell.

There is no real magic trick to charisma, though. Basically, it is the ability to instill enthusiasm in others. Think back to the last time you were in the presence of such a charismatic dynamo. Were you not energized by his enthusiastic nature? Did the bright light of his life not draw you closer? We are all attracted to those who embody the pure essence of a zealous existence. However, charisma does not imply a hyperactive personality or a person of overwhelming intensity. It is simply a contagious spirit of optimism and enthusiasm.

We can begin cultivating a charismatic personality by developing a dream. When we share a goal that taps into the dreams and desires of others, we create a vision worthy of pursuit. By attacking this ambition with unwavering determination and intensity, others will feel inspired to join in the crusade. People will follow a charismatic leader, drawn by his enthusiastic belief in total victory. Think of all the great charitable organizations and worthy causes started by such an individual. What an incredible image of success!

"If you learn to believe in yourself, it is natural for others to believe in you."
- Lynn Tincher, author of Afterthoughts
www.lynntincher.com

All the excitement in the world will not conceal an uncaring attitude, though. We must love and appreciate those around us as well. When others can sense in us a genuine understanding and acceptance, they feel secure. They are drawn by the promise of a trusted relationship. A true steward of the people does not need to lord over his subjects, dangling approval as if it were a reward for submission. He is personable and genuinely cares for the well being of his followers.

As history has proven, people will not willingly follow an individual they fear. Threats and demands might buy supporters, but such behavior does not instill loyalty. The image of a ruthless tyrant is not one people will revere and honor. It certainly lacks genuine charisma! And without the honest qualities of a charismatic leader, it will be impossible for such a person to earn long-term respect.

A success image implies that our actions back up our words. We do exactly as promised and accomplish tasks in a timely manner. This type of individual is often known as someone who 'gets things done'. Even more important, he is honest and upholds his end of the bargain. His superiors and followers rely on his steadfast and consistent nature. We can cultivate this level of respect as well by following through on our declarations and promises.

Accomplished leaders exhibit not only consistency in their dealings but a certain amount of flexibility, too. They make no rash or imprudent decisions but are quick to decide. In the heat of battle, they are calm but energized. These assessments may appear to be a contradiction in terms, but mastering paradoxes is part of a successful individual's makeup. The victorious maneuvering of such a fine line speaks volumes. As long as we do not become rigid in our choices and hold a Plan B in reserve, we will present this image, too.

One misconception regarding successful people stems from the belief they are all of high intelligence. While this is often true, the aspects of wisdom and cleverness play a critical role. A sharp leader doesn't need to know everything; he just needs to know where to locate the knowledge. He wisely surrounds himself with bright, intellectual minds, providing him with a vast wealth of knowledge and information. Therefore, it is not required that we appear the brightest bulbs in the hallway. We simply need friends who are that bright!

A trait occasionally forgotten when climbing the ladder of success is the courtesy of manners. Remember to say please and thank you. Do not keep people waiting unless absolutely necessary. Extend greetings and considerate offers whenever possible. These polite and respectful gestures are necessary touches on a charismatic personality.

To complete the success image, always play on your strengths. Recognize your weaknesses, but do not focus on these shortcomings. Remember, you threw away that list of bad habits in the previous chapter! Do not revisit those negative imperfections. Develop confidence in your abilities and allow the strengths to shine.

Developing charisma and mastering paradoxes might appear a daunting task. Do not shy away from success just because you don't feel as if you will fit the image. Create the image! Dress and act appropriately, and pursue goals with passion and enthusiasm. If you just keep moving forward, one day you will glance back and be amazed at your progress!

In a nutshell...
- Dress for success
- Develop a charismatic personality
- Love and appreciate others
- Be consistent and yet flexible
- Surround yourself with intelligent people
- Don't forget your manners

22

Real Criticism is an Art

If you don't have something good to say, don't say anything at all. It's a good motto, but regrettably, some people still feel the urge to proudly present belittling nuggets of negative. Sometimes the best thing these individuals can offer is an example of why nobody likes a critic! However, those residing in a position of authority will occasionally find criticism unavoidable. The best course of action is to master the art of constructive criticism.

Why is a chapter on criticizing and belittling necessary in the section covering self-esteem? These behaviors factor into our self-image. Contrary to what some people believe, we cannot raise our self-esteem by disparaging others. Putting down other people does not make us look better, nor does it help our self-image. Not surprisingly, our self-esteem rises instead when we build up our friends, family and co-workers. Therefore, if we are called to criticize, we must learn to do so without depreciating the value of other people.

First, we must define criticism on a basic and practical level. We are all quite familiar with movie critics and their ability to rake a film across the coals. These individuals appear to revel in their power to condemn a movie to box office disaster. However, the true purpose of criticism is not to tear down but build up character and content. To truly critique is to offer suggestions and possible improvements. Therefore, criticism should only be conducted in the spirit of assistance and encouragement.

One way to temper critical words is to recall how we feel when on the receiving end of such harsh comments. When someone offers negative criticism coupled with inconsiderate intensions, are we encouraged or discouraged? Is it the tone of voice, the method of delivery, the actual words, or a combination of all three that dampens our spirits? Most of us are not receptive to such criticism, as the attack feels quite personal. We would all fare better to remember such emotions, though, especially the next time we are faced with the task of criticizing another person.

There is a proper time and place for voicing such judgments as well. Criticism should be performed in private whenever possible. Examining another's shortcomings in front of his friends or peers often causes embarrassment and humiliation for that individual. Those gathered will also feel uncomfortable and ill at ease. Too often, trust is eroded when followers or friends fear a public attack. Such disregard for the feelings of others will likely create many new enemies, too!

Instead, select a place and time when the matter can be discussed without an audience. This will also provide time to gather thoughts and plan an approach to the problem. For those who tend to react out of anger, this helps to curb emotional and impulsive behavior, too. The other person will appreciate this gesture of consideration and feel more at ease in a private setting.

There is also proper and thoughtful procedure to present criticism. Sandwiching judgments between words of praise lessens the negative impact and causes the recipient to feel more receptive to the criticism. Regardless of the issue in question, we can always find something of value in another human being! By expressing approval of other behaviors or efforts, we supply that individual with a platform on which to build future success.

Criticism should always be directed at the issue, not the individual. Condemning someone personally only causes his defenses to rise. Once the wall goes up, further conversation will fall on deaf ears. Focus instead on the problem and offer solutions in the analysis.

Even in private, a person may feel embarrassed when his mistakes are revealed. Rather than force him into a corner, allow him a quiet means of escaping the situation. Perhaps he was unaware of the problem or lacked the correct information. Give the person the opportunity to save face rather than force him to admit that he erred. You will earn more respect following this path, not to mention make future confrontations easier to handle.

Real problems can arise if we attempt to rub someone's face in a mistake. This is not criticism but outright punishment, and it will cause the opposite desired effect. Humiliation does not inspire a person to perform better or work harder! The individual receiving such treatment will feel only resentment and perceive the criticism as a personal attack. Remember, human nature dictates that he will dig in his heels and absolutely refuse to change or correct the problem. Beating down those with low self-esteem also causes their self-image to degenerate even further, thus perpetuating the pattern of mistakes. No one performs well with a crushed ego.

Tempering all critical comments with compassion garners far greater results! Instilling fear or using force tends to hurt production and performance. When dealing with personal relationships, it might even mean the loss of a friendship. Thoughtful criticism demonstrates respect and feeds rather than starves an individual's self-esteem.

People rise to meet the expectations placed before them. Believe they will make improvements and then honestly convey this conviction. Expect others to work harder and to act in a trustworthy manner. If convinced of this sincere belief, most will move mountains to meet such expectations!

However, heed this word of caution concerning high expectations. Occasionally a goal is truly out of reach for an individual. The expectations may fall outside of that person's physical capabilities or reside beyond his level of skill. Repeated failed attempts will gradually chip away at his self-esteem. Recognize when a task is too great for someone and shift the responsibility to another person if necessary. In the case of personal relationships, sometimes situations arise where good intentions simply weren't enough. Better to change expectations or discover another option than ruin a friendship.

Harsh criticisms never result in a positive outcome. However, if we temper our criticisms with compassion, offer praise and encouragement, we will motivate others to great achievements. The boost to our self-esteem far outweighs any other solution, too.

In a nutshell...
- Criticism affects both giver and recipient
- The purpose of criticism is to build up
- Criticism should always be performed in private
- Learn to sandwich judgments between praise
- Forcing others to admit guilt does not work
- People rise to meet expectations

23

Moving Past Barriers

Our self-esteems are in constant fluctuation. Situations continually arise that cause an increase or reduction in the level. The goal is to avoid the drastic drops and move past barriers and obstacles. This means we need to work on building and protecting our self-esteem every single day!

Every human on earth faces challenges. Even Jesus dealt with difficulties! No one's life is perfect. We will always encounter opposition and problems that slow our progress. However, obstacles should never stop our growth. Troubles should not be allowed to decrease our self-esteem, either.

Mistakes will be made, but the key is to learn from these setbacks and stumbling blocks. Errors should be viewed as opportunities to grow and change. When we fail to learn, our self-image receives a blow. Mistakes that appear minor can simply devastate us if we allow them to halt all forward progress. Don't allow something as small as a pebble to cause a fall. Stand up, dust off, and remember we are greater than any earthly problem. Besides, if no one will care in a hundred years, then neither should we!

People can sometimes be just as great a problem. If you've been verbally attacked or experienced a confrontation recently then you will agree with that assessment! Protect your self-esteem from the negative input of others. Do not allow anyone to tear you down verbally, physically or emotionally. Quickly remove yourself from the presence of such individuals and limit further contact.

On some occasions, negative people will be unavoidable. In the case of co-workers and family members, you can only hide for so long! Simply don your mental armor and let their words bounce off your mind. The less time you dwell upon their comment, the less negative will creep into your heart and challenge your self-image. If you don't take the implied insults and insinuations personal, then it will be as if water off a duck's back.

To counter the effects of such negative individuals, seek the company of those you admire and trust. If you are struggling with challenges, these people can offer encouragement or assistance. The feedback and positive input you are likely to receive will help you to remain proactive and rejuvenate your thought process. This stimulus might be all you require to remain focused and positive until a solution is discovered. Discouragement and despair will not have an opportunity to deplete your self-esteem.

Reality is all a matter of perception in our minds. Instead of merely hoping for success, speak as if it were already true. A car salesman with a goal of moving fifteen cars a month should not say that is what he wants, he should say it's already an accomplishment. If a man desires to exercise thirty minutes every day, he should say that he is actively doing it right now. It is not a lie, but an attempt to inform the brain of the desired reality. Our minds are so powerful, they will begin to conform to such a reality and make it happen!

Sounds crazy doesn't it? However, positive self-talk really works. We are reprogramming our minds for success. By telling our brain the desired result, it goes to work and takes steps toward that goal. As we slowly move toward our target, we enjoy small accomplishments. Every time we experience these little victories, our self-esteem rises. As our self-image grows, so does our confidence, and we are willing to continue taking steps toward our ultimate goal. It's the vicious cycle, only with a positive twist! We accomplish this through the power of words of affirmation, just as the Bible says to speak and we shall move mountains.

Within those pages is also the story of the talents and the idea of use it or lose it. We all possess talents and strengths upon which we should focus. If we do not exercise such gifts, those abilities diminish in effectiveness. We should not envy another's capability or attempt to duplicate his results exactly. While our friend might choose one course of action, our strengths will likely take us on a different path to reach the intended target. As long as it is moral, ethical, and legal, there is more than one way to skin a cat! We are to concentrate on our talents and find our own route to success.

Remember stretching in gym class? We were taught to stretch before attempting strenuous activity. Carry this thought process and basic principal into goal-setting as well. Take many small steps before making that giant leap. Failure due to sights set too high leads to discouragement. Provide the ego with the opportunity to build, and stretch a little every day. Small successes will develop a secure and strong self-esteem.

OVERCOMING

"Living life is sometimes like mountain climbing; you fight an uphill battle one foot at a time striving for that ultimate almost un-achieving final step at the top, where you look back at your endeavors and feel success."
Nick B. Comande, Firefighter. Author of Climbing for Causes
www.climbingforcauses.org

OBSTACLES

Life's challenges can overwhelm us completely when we are exhausted. The world in which we reside can grow very hectic. Time constraints can eventually squeeze our very soul. Our energy wanes, judgments turn questionable, and emotional control grows difficult. We simply cannot perform our best when exhausted. As we begin to drag, so does our self-esteem.

Like a battery, we must occasionally recharge. Allowing for a full night's sleep or periods of rest during the day is vitally important. A little extra sleep is good for a tired body. Don't forget that our minds require energizing as well. Senses grow dull when there are no new stimuli on which to feed. Provide the brain with a change of scenery and a break, too. Once rested and refreshed, we can attack our problems anew.

Since confidence grows shaky when we cannot solve a problem, our self-esteem will also begin to slide. Rather than feel frustrated by what is perceived as an insurmountable barrier, set the challenge aside for a moment. Instead, tackle a new activity- one in which it is possible to excel! By achieving a measure of success, even in something as simple as gardening or a sport, we feel invigorated and our confidence grows. Armed with this fresh victory, we'll feel prepared to take on life's challenges once again.

As in nature, balance promotes growth and harmony. We as humans must maintain balance in our lives as well. We can still pursue ambitions with passion and intensity, but these aspirations cannot represent our entire existence. Pursuing a single goal for an extended period of time, (while ignoring all else), often results in an even greater loss than failing to capture that target. The man who spends his entire waking hours at work will soon discover he has no family awaiting his return!

Balance does not mean all parts of our life are equally matched, like a perfectly sliced apple pie. Equilibrium is achieved when all areas receive adequate attention. Each portion requires a different level of time commitment, but all segments are important to the whole of our life. Remember, no one earthly person or object will make us happy! We require a multitude of elements in our life to feel true joy and peace.

Temporary barriers should not become permanent walls. No matter what we face, there is always a solution and people who have triumphed before us. Helen Keller never allowed her 'handicaps' to destroy her self-esteem or prevent her from pursuing her goals. What's our excuse?

In a nutshell...
- Everyone faces challenges in life
- Learn from mistakes and avoid negative people
- Speak success as if it were already real
- Focus on your talents and strengths
- Recharge your mind
- Maintain balance

Key 4

Overcoming Fears

The greatest obstacle facing success is fear. No other single force prevents us from accomplishing our goals as effectively as this negative emotion. It controls and binds as if we were prisoners.

To conquer this great demoralizer, we must recognize and understand all facets of fear, eventually gaining the strength to overcome. If we are to achieve our full potential, we must be willing to take risks despite our fears.

This brings us to the fourth Key- overcoming fear!

24

The Truth About Fear

Every human on earth has experienced fear. It creeps into our lives and paralyzes our bodies and minds. What is the purpose of this strong, negative emotion and from where does it originate?

Author and coach, David Ambrose, has this to say on the truth about fear:

The chilling, unmistakable roar of a saber-toothed tiger outside his cave propels the caveman to grab his weapons and get outside to face his first threat of the day. The sudden stab of fear gets his adrenaline pumping with each beat of his heart. He is intensely alert to every nuance of his surroundings, as he darts out to defend his home and his family...

Thankfully, this is a kind of fear most of us will never experience.

Of all our feelings, fear is both one of the most vital for our survival and at the same time the most destructive. Indeed, without fear, we would never have evolved to become the intelligent, thinking beings we are today. We would have become extinct thousands of years ago.

Over the years, I have discovered that there is one thing, and only one thing that stands in the way of us achieving our potential, and that is fear. Every negative thing we feel has fear as its foundation. Whatever it is, anger, guilt, loneliness, sadness, inadequacy, stress...all are rooted in fear.

The 1930s were an intensely bleak time for America as the depression ravaged the entire country. When he took office in 1933, FDR gave his famous inaugural and spoke about fear: "...let me assert my firm belief that the only thing we have to fear is fear itself—nameless, unreasoning, unjustified terror which paralyzes needed efforts to convert retreat into advance." In saying this, FDR clearly illustrated the power fear has over the unwary.

Have you ever wondered why we feel fear? Let's look at what fear is all about. Back when the caveman was suddenly rudely awaken, fear was an important component of his toolbox for survival. The purpose of fear has always been to warn us of the possibility of danger...it gives us a warning to take whatever action is necessary to survive when danger threatens—whether it is to fight off an attacking saber-toothed tiger outside our cave, or sharpening our senses for the impending attack of a futuristic cyborg in a computer game.

Fear has the effect of changing our body chemistry, boosting adrenalin to give us the focus and energy necessary to save ourselves. Interestingly, we feel more alive when we feel this kind of fear; this is why people flock to see horror movies, and probably why some people get hooked on extreme sports.

Not all fear serves us as well as it did our cave dwelling ancestors, though. Indeed, for most of our modern-day lives, the original purpose of fear is superfluous—just like our appendix.

Fear builds upon itself, often growing way out of proportion; and yet most of the time, the things we fear never come to pass...and when they do, the effect is almost never as severe as we had envisioned. Statistics indicate that 94% of the things we worry about never happen. Imagine not generating all that negative energy worrying about things that *could* happen, but almost certainly won't!

If we were to dig down to the root causes behind all the violence and conflict in the world today, we would likely find fear right there in the number one spot. It may be fear of loss, fear of ridicule, fear of rejection, fear of isolation, fear of commitment, fear of appearing weak; whatever it is, one of our fears is there.

We have little or no control over most of the things that *are* worth worrying about. There is nothing we can directly do about threats like nuclear war, terrorist attacks, bird flu, or whatever other fearsome threat the press decides to focus on this week, so how do we benefit by living in fear?

This isn't to say that we should be complacent about potential dangers or threats like global warming, but we should keep it all in perspective. Most fear does not help us. Remember, fear's purpose is to galvanize us to take action.

Even though it is often unproductive, we all experience fear, even our heroes and people who may seem outwardly impervious to it have their moments of fear. The true test is how we react when we come face to face with it...but before we can face it, we have to recognize it. This is not always as obvious as it may seem.

Fear (as we experience it today) is learned, and encouraged from several directions. It is a far cry from the sudden adrenaline-creating fear that a saber toothed tiger at your door would induce. It is far more prevalent and insidious than you may think.

Let me explain. In advertising, one of the first things prospective copywriters are taught is that there are essentially two reasons why people buy things: The first is to reduce their pain; the other is to increase their pleasure. If you think about it, these are really two sides of the same coin.

It has further been found that people will part with their money more easily when promised something to reduce their pain, than they will for something to increase their pleasure. In practical terms, it is easier for marketers to fan the flames of fear than it is to relieve pain, so they substitute the word pain, with fear.

Looking at the advertisements we are exposed to daily, with a little practice it is easy to identify which fear is being fed. Here are a couple of random examples:

· Antiseptic wipes- feeds the fear of sickness and death; and the fear of being perceived as a bad parent...even though our forebears survived for millennia without them.

· Tooth whiteners and a host of other personal products and cosmetics- feed the fear of rejection, and of appearing ugly, plain, too thin, or too fat... playing on our need to fit in and be accepted.

Even without these *manufactured* fears, fear is a large part of our upbringing and is part of every aspect of life.

When we were children, our parents used fear to protect us from dangers they perceived, whether they were real or imagined. Religions use fear of retribution and damnation to keep their congregations in line, and governments learned long ago that an ignorant and fearful populace is far more pliable than one that is well informed and feeling secure. History abounds with examples of rulers using, or creating, fear to achieve their objectives, often at the expense of the people they were supposed to serve...and it continues around the planet even today.

On a social level, we have an instinctual desire to be accepted by our community. This is how peer pressure works; we fear discrimination and rejection, which are the consequences of being seen as too different. We have seen others ridiculed or shunned because of their looks, race, status, gender, size, or some other indication that they don't fit the mold of those around them, and we can go to great lengths to avoid being in that position.

For a few days, think about this and try to identify all the messages you receive that are designed to generate fear of something or someone. You will be amazed at how many there actually are on any given day.

The key to overcoming fear is to recognize it, and then heed its original purpose; to acknowledge it, and then take action to remove it. To use FDR's words, we will then be able to "convert retreat into advance" and achieve our full potential as individuals and as part of our community.

- David Ambrose has developed a number of projects aimed at helping people find enduring happiness based on his own search for happiness. This personal quest resulted in his award winning book "Your Life Manual: Practical Steps to Genuine Happiness" in 2006. He recently published another book based on his successful series of "Happiness Minutes" and continues working to promote lasting happiness and life fulfillment. For more details - www.YourLifeManual.com, www.HappinessMinute.com

Fear is a universal feeling, one shared by all living creatures. Now that we understand the facts, we can work on identifying and conquering our fears. Remember, knowledge of fear is only power when acted upon!

In a nutshell...
- All negative feelings are rooted in fear
- Fear is a fight or flight response
- Almost all worries never occur
- Many fears today are manufactured
- Recognize and take action against fear

25

Facets of Fear

Before we can overcome and conquer fear, we must understand its many facets. Fear comes in many forms and elicits a variety of reactions. Once we recognize these various forms and understand the underlying causes and reasons for each one, we will be better equipped to deal with our fears.

Humans are born possessing only two fears. We fear falling and loud noises. All others are a learned behavior. We acquire fears as we experience life's many situations and people.

Many anxieties are inherited when we are children, either from our parents or other close contacts. A mother's fear of bridges might translate into a similar fear in her children. If we were never taught to swim, we might feel apprehensive toward water. Even prejudice, which qualifies as a fear of the unknown, can be passed from parents to children.

Other fears are learned through experience. A traumatic ordeal in front of a crowd of people can develop into a fear of public speaking. If a large dog knocks us down when we are very young, we might grow up to fear dogs in general. Negative experiences such as these contribute to the development of many fears. Often the original episode was not as traumatic as we recall, but the moment sticks in our minds. Over time, our brain exaggerates the experience, further fueling our fear.

Failure resides at the core of almost all fears. We are terrified of failing on every level: emotionally, intellectually, and physically. Failure questions our worth and value as a human being.

Since we crave acceptance and approval, unsuccessful attempts to acquire these things devastates our self-image.

Society places an enormous amount of emphasis on winning. There is incredible pressure on us to succeed at all costs. We watch sporting events where there can only be one winner. At work, we are told we must perform perfectly if we are to advance. Schools place emphasis on passing tests and grades. All around us, we hear that we must succeed, or we'll be considered a loser and a failure. We must win right now!

However, nothing could be further from the truth. Life continues beyond this moment in time and there is always another opportunity for success in the future. (A football game may be a one-time occurrence, but there will be other games.) In everyday life, we are given many opportunities, and we can continue to reach for our goals. The only real obstacle between our dreams and us is death! However, even dying is not considered failure.

Real failure comes when we cease to try. If we endeavor to prevail in our efforts, the only way we can truly fail is if we abandon our pursuit. Think of all the attempts by Edison to create the light bulb. One might say he failed over ten thousand times, but since he stayed the course, that final, successful attempt is all that is important. Therefore, it is not how many times we try that matters. As long as we do not give up, we are not defeated.

Failing is a deep-rooted emotional fear. It damages our self-esteem and wrecks havoc on our feelings. Some failure fears are valid, as they could result in bodily harm. Failure at rock climbing, fighting fires, or rattlesnake handling could result in serious injury or death. Those fears are actually protecting our lives. A fear of failure that ends with embarrassment or discouragement has nothing to do with physical harm, though. Ironically, it is these intangible consequences, felt only in the mind, that we seem to fear the most.

The basic fear of failing is present in all facets of fear. From a fear of snakes to the trauma of being turned down for a date, all are connected to losing in some manner. Blows that damage the self-esteem are just as devastating as losing one's life or receiving injury, too. As we will see though, all fears feel real to the mind, regardless of the threat involved.

Remarkably enough, some people fear success itself. This may appear contrary to the belief that fear stems from failure anxiety. Yet with success in any endeavor comes the expectation to repeat that action. For many individuals, this pressure translates into fear. An advancement in position at the company sounds inviting, but with it comes a new level of commitment and responsibility as well. This terrifies and creates panic in some people. They feel the expectations and pressure will be too great. This fear of success will either prevent them from moving into the position or cause paralysis in their new placement.

Fear can prevent us from taking action. We may desire a goal but feel afraid to take the first step. Often we rationalize and offer reasons for our inactivity, but fear is what truly holds us fast. Our friends may tackle the rock wall at the state fair, but our anxiety means we remain on the ground. We may want to finally acquire our college degree, but fear prevents us from returning to school. The action required appears frightening and we feel incapable of even moving.

Many fear occurrences are simply a part of life. How many people do we know who fear death? We have no control over aging or dying, and yet it terrifies a good portion of the human race. Illness is another occurrence over which we sometimes have no control, despite all effort to remain healthy. Think of all the people who spend nine months fretting over their impending parenthood! These fears all stem from events that are often just the natural course of life and beyond our ability to control.

Fear of failure is most apparent in the fear of rejection. Approval and acceptance are basic human needs and when our ideas and proposals are refused or denied, it damages our self-esteem. We feel like a failure. Rejection itself can come in many forms-being turned down for a date; our suggestion or offer is declined; acceptance to a particular college is denied; and so forth. Rather than risk receiving a rejection, many fail to make any attempt.

Rejection is difficult to handle because it feels personal, as if our value and worth has been discredited. However, a negative response often has little to do with us. The timing may simply not be right. A rejection might be the result of a random selection and our number was not chosen. When a rejection is received from an individual, it often has more to do with that person's current frame of mind than a fault or lack within us. If we were to remove our ego from the equation, then the fear of rejection loses much of its power. No one enjoys rejection, but we certainly don't have to take it personal, either!

In the corner opposite of fear resides faith. When we consider all existing fears, this truth becomes obvious. Faith is belief. It is a sense of hope and confidence. Fears arise when we harbor doubt. The person who hesitates entering a race doubts his ability to run fast enough. The man afraid to ask a beautiful woman out on a date does not believe she will find him attractive or desirable. Neither of these individuals possesses faith in their abilities.

OVERCOMING

"The best antidote for fear is faith. The focus of fear is looking at the power of a problem. The focus of faith is looking at the solution to the problem. Fear has the power to drive out faith and faith has the power to drive out fear! The most powerful one is the one you ultimately yield to."
- Bill Wilson, author & Pastor of The Lord's Table

OBSTACLES

If we remove the doubt and replace it with faith, then there is no reason to feel afraid. Fear loses all of its power! By focusing on faith and belief, we see past the 'what if' scenarios. We see the potential victory instead. The unknown can appear daunting, but by removing doubt, we come to realize we can indeed handle the situation. If we knew for certain that we could handle these fearful situations, would we still fear them? Our list of fears grows very short when we think and believe in this manner.

Fear was designed to preserve our lives, not hold us prisoner. By understanding fear's many facets, we can take the first step toward our freedom.

In a nutshell...
- Almost all fears are learned
- At the core is the fear of failure
- Failure only occurs when we cease to try
- Fear prevents us from taking action
- Do not take rejection personal
- Remove doubt and replace it with faith

26

Breaking the Fear Barrier

Now we recognize and understand fear as it looms over us. How do we go about battling the beast, though? What is required to break through this invisible barrier?

Author Jocelyn Andersen provides us with an incredible, real-life example of how fear can be broken: (Reprinted with permission from Jocelyn Andersen's book, *Woman Submit! Christians & Domestic Violence.*)

My journey from fear to peace was a long and painful one. And I do not know of any short cuts. I can only share from my own experience that when I finally reached the point of saturation—the point at which I could tolerate no more fear or pain—I finally became willing to give up my methods of dealing with the problems within my marriage and allowed God to begin teaching me his. It was then that I began desperately crying out to God for new direction—and, as always, he answered me.

It was not the answer I was looking for. But it was definitely the answer I needed. It was at that point in my life that I discovered God's blueprint for freedom—Proverbs 2:10-13 (covered in detail in chapter five). I knew God had spoken to me through this passage of scripture. And after studying it closely, I began to understand what truly remarkable and concise direction it gave. I knew I had reached a turning point in my life, and if I could learn to implement the instruction I had just received, I could be free, forever, from the torment of indecision and from fear of losing my spouse.

That passage helped me understand that when I became willing to see and do things God's way instead of my way, I would be cared for by God and would no longer be at the mercy of abusive treatment or threats of abandonment.

Did that understanding solve the problems within my marriage? No. Did I immediately run out and file for divorce? To my family's everlasting dismay, no, I did not. It took quite some time for me to firmly grasp the fact that I had to let go of the wheel. I had to give up control. I had to stop trying to figure everything out.

Is that a surprising statement coming from one who was trying to escape *being* controlled? It shouldn't. Everyone has to have some sense that they are in control of some portion of their lives. One of my ways of feeling in control of that chaotic situation was by not admitting defeat. I simply refused to give up. I was constantly trying to figure out ways to fix things. I was even using prayer to try and control the situation. That was wrong.

It was with great difficulty that I reached the painful conclusion that my efforts to change my beloved abuser might be fruitless. And I finally, reluctantly, became willing to accept the consequence of divorce or permanent separation if that became necessary.

I would like to stop here and say that I am not advocating divorce as an across-the-board solution for all marriages with these types of problems. I am saying though, that painful as it may be, the possibility of divorce or permanent separation must become a viable option to the abused or battered wife. The *possibility* of divorce or permanent separation must cease to become the unthinkable if she ever hopes to be free from fear of these things.

We cannot be threatened with things we do not fear.

Over the next few years, through many separations and reconciliations, I made repeated sincere efforts to save my marriage, but my efforts finally boiled down to simply trying to free myself emotionally, physically, and legally from my husband.

I admit there were many occasions when I initiated a separation in an effort to manipulate my husband into seeking professional help. Did it work? Sometimes—temporarily. Other times

I left in an effort to be free from him forever. Did that work? Over a period of time—yes.

There are those who still criticize me for loving my abusive husband and "wasting" years of my life trying to make that marriage work. The following are a few of the questions I wrestled with as I struggled to find some sanity and God-given solutions to the chaos that filled my life, and some conclusions I finally came to:

- Is it ok for an abused wife to love her husband? Yes.
- Is it ok to want to make the marriage work? Yes.
- Is it ok to leave if the abuse escalates? Yes.
- Is it ok to return and try again? As much as I would love to say, "*No! Stay away,*" the answer to that question has to be yes as well.

Can any of us definitively say that it is *always* the will of God for an abused wife to leave her husband permanently? No, we cannot. But we *can* definitively say that if she acknowledges God in all her ways, he *will* direct her paths. We *can* definitively say we know it is within the parameters of God's perfect will, as revealed in his written word, for an abused wife to proactively seek ways to protect herself from assault and abuse.

We can assure an abused wife that it is not okay to be motivated, coerced, and seemingly driven into returning by fear, guilt, false hope, and confusion. The scriptures tell us the wisdom that comes from above (from God) is peaceable, gentle, and easy to be received. God leads. He does not drive. And he is *not* the author of confusion.

But if a woman is acknowledging God in all her ways, and feels the Holy Spirit is directing her path and leading her not to end her marriage, or even continue with a separation—as much as that may gall the rest of us—her choices need to be acknowledged as valid. She may indeed be following the leading of the Holy Spirit. Who are we to say she is not?

In my case, though, I eventually reached the point where I could deal with the possibility of losing my husband without the fear and pain it had previously produced. I accepted the fact that he might never change. That in turn made it possible for me to take off the rose-colored glasses and see my marriage for what it really was, rather than how I wanted to see it.

I came to realize the fine-tuner on my discernment apparatus had become damaged due to constant exposure to abuse. As the fear abated, it began working again, and I began seeing things differently. In addition to the overt abuse, I found the covert and more subtle abuse in our marriage coming into sharper focus. For the first time in a very long time I was seeing things clearly. I could honestly face the fact that I had developed a tolerance for the abuse and could admit that I had been accepting much of it without challenge.

- Jocelyn Andersen is an expert media commentator on issues related to domestic violence and Christian response. She is the author of four books including, Woman Submit! Christians & Domestic Violence. www.JocelynAndersen.com

Breaking the fear barrier occurs when we reach the point of absolution. We are aware of the fear and its control on our lives. Once we can clearly see this reality, we are finally able to take the next step.

In a nutshell...
- We must recognize fear's hold
- Sometimes fear resides in all directions
- Fear blinds us to the truth
- When we hit saturation, everything grows clear
- Breaking the barrier is just the beginning

27

Take Action to Cure Fear

Acting upon a fear does not sound appealing. It's probably the last thing we desire! That does not change the truth of the matter, though. We can only conquer fear by facing it and taking action.

Every person on earth experiences fear. No one is immune. Yet, for every anxiety we possess, someone in this world has faced and overcome that concern. That should give us hope! The good news is that once we take action, the fear dwindles. It's the very first step that's always the most difficult. If we can just do it once, conquer fear only one time, then the next time it is easier to accomplish the task. It is vital then that we take the first step.

"Fear is an evil little monster. With a little determination, you can defeat it."
- Lynn Tincher, author of Afterthoughts
www.lynntincher.com

All fear is not created equal, and often our anxiety is quite unjustified. Over ninety percent of all worries never even happen. If nine out of ten concerns are pointless, then why waste the time and energy worrying? Such trepidation simply steals our future and present joy. It also removes the goal from our sight and halts foreword progress. We must not allow such worry to consume us then.

If we were to write down all of our fears and concerns, we'd discover more than one possible scenario for each item on the list. We might even realize a few are rather ridiculous and utterly impossible! Obviously, all of these results cannot happen at the same time. It is likely none of these situations will arise or come true. Therefore, why waste time worrying about every item on that list? Our energy and brainpower would be better spent elsewhere. We need to use that vivid imagination to conjure up images of success not fear!

Sometimes we hesitate to take action because we expect all of the conditions to be just right. We envision only one option for overcoming our fear, and if everything doesn't align perfectly with our plan, we refuse to take action. The young man waiting for the moment when the object of his desire is alone before approaching her might discover that her friends never leave her side. He will need to adjust his approach or expectations if he hopes to ask the young woman on a date!

Circumstances rarely line up just the way we envisioned. We must either alter our plan or create the proper situation that will ensure our success. In the example of the young man, he does have options. If he's determined to speak to the young lady alone, he can always ask her friends for a moment of privacy. Many times changing the circumstances to fit our needs is that simple, but we become so fixated on the obstacles that we fail to seek other solutions. This is when we need to employ that vivid imagination!

We often place too much emphasis on the process and too little on the results. What matters more, Edison's many attempts or the final effort to create the light bulb? The failed experiments do not matter, only the accomplishment! As long as our approach is moral, ethical and legal, only the end result is important. Unlike the game of baseball, we are not automatically out after three unsuccessful swings.

What happens when the fear involves making a decision? We run the risk of making the wrong decision! However, unless human life really is involved, it is doubtful anyone will die if we make a less than perfect choice. If our decision involves such heavy and serious consequences, then we certainly must weigh our options carefully. Rarely is the decision that momentous, though. The dire consequences we usually envision in our mind are fueled only by fear.

The answer is simple- step up and make a decision! If it's not the best choice, then learn from the results and try again. That's how we develop and grow. A poor decision is only detrimental if we allow it to stop us dead in our tracks. As we often hear, what's the worst that can happen? Lest we forget, failure to make a decision means we've made a passive choice. Make an active decision instead.

The first step will also appear very frightening if we have not prepared for the situation. Whether our attempt is successful or not, we must be ready for the results. Fearing the first step because we won't know what to do if we succeed or fail is a poor excuse for inaction. Occasionally we may have to take a blind leap of faith, and that is fine if we are capable of the feat. However, if the landing is obscured, then perhaps a little pre-planning is in order. Sometimes we do need to look before we leap. Just do not allow this stage to develop into a resting place!

In some cases, a little preparation makes all the difference in the world. Many people list public speaking as one of their greatest fears and shun every instance to perform this action. Leadership positions often require a certain level of public speaking, however. It is a fear that must be conquered and preparation can mean the difference between a glowing accomplishment and a dismal attempt.

OVERCOMING

"Do you realize that almost everyone approaches public speaking with butterflies in their stomach? The secret is to get those butterflies to fly in formation. To do that, have notes and know just what you want to say. Pick one person in the audience and talk just to them. And it's okay to admit that you're nervous. That always puts the audience on your side."
Austin S. Camacho, author of the Hannibal Jones Mysteries
www.ascamacho.com

OBSTACLES

There are several options available to us before tackling this fear. Several organizations provide training in the area of public speaking. Members of these groups create and perform practice speeches that are then critiqued by the others. Additionally, there are often college courses or free programs available to the public. Any of these options will improve our speaking skills within a few months. We should also research the group to whom we will speak before the event, especially if it is outside of our own organization. If we understand our listeners, we can better address their needs.

Why is it so vitally important that we take action? The day we stop risking failure, we hit the glass ceiling in terms of our potential. We reach our maximum achievement level. In this situation, we cannot grow as leaders or individuals. In nature, objects are either growing and changing or stagnant and dying. When we cease to take risks in life, we stagnate as people. The only way we can achieve more is to stretch beyond our comfort zone and actively conquer our fears.

Fear can only hold us prisoner if we fail to act. Our fears are not as daunting as they appear and will hold little meaning in the end. The sooner we begin tackling these obstacles, the sooner we can break free of their influence. Take control, take action, and conquer those fears today!

In a nutshell...
- Everyone experiences and feels fear
- Most worries never happen
- Circumstances will never be perfect
- Make a decision- any decision
- Prepare for the situation
- Continue taking risks or risk stagnating

28

Organization and Confidence

When we lack confidence or life throws us into a state of disorganization, the result is a feeling of uncertainty. This in turn paralyzes and prevents further action. If we are to become an effective leader, we must master organization, act with confidence, and instill these behaviors in our followers.

These two qualities are entwined. If we are unorganized, we do not give others confidence in our abilities. Our lack of confidence is occasionally due in part to misinformation or poor planning. One trait affects the other. How well we portray these attributes will have a profound effect on others as well.

A leader who lacks confidence and organizational skills usually finds the devotion of his followers in question. When those in charge appear scatterbrained and uncertain, it's cause for concern in the ranks! We are wary of poor decisions, hesitation and a lack of coordination. The leader must display confidence on par with his position and back it up with structure if he hopes to retain respect. Not only will people be more inclined to follow someone with these traits, they will develop similar attributes as well.

Confidence and assurance arise when we are comfortable in our position. We feel at ease when we understand and possess knowledge on all necessary topics. This is where organizational skills play a key role in leadership. If we fail to gather sufficient information, we are unable to properly perform our duties. The resulting feeling of inadequacy leads to a drop in confidence. How can we act if we don't know what we are doing? Good organizational habits are necessary for leaders and anyone in pursuit of accomplishment.

Some of us are blessed with natural abilities in this area. We maintain a structured schedule, arrange our time wisely, and have a system in place. If someone calls wanting details on a project three years old, we can lay our hands on the information within seconds. We are the masters of the daily routine and maintain such order in all aspects of life. For organized individuals, it is almost effortless!

However, if disarray and confusion better describes our day, then effort will be required. The person who can scarcely locate his car keys, let alone an old file, will need to develop some organization skills. Even the most uncoordinated and disorderly individual can make some improvements.

Some tips for developing organizational skills:

- Make a to-do list and prioritize
- Allow sufficient time for all activities
- Purchase a calendar or PDA and use it
- Devote time to research & preparation
- File or return items to original location immediately
- Do not tackle too much- know when to say no
- Learn to delegate duties
- Recognize and limit distractions
- Refuse to procrastinate

As our organizational skills increase, so will our confidence, and we will gain our follower's confidence as well. The mirror effect is very strong in this area. If we act confident, it will instill assurance in others. And similar to developing enthusiasm, sometimes we have to fake it until we make it!

A bold and certain spirit also increases decisiveness. Without fear and doubt clouding our judgment, we are able to make and stick with decisions. Waffling does not inspire the troops! They need an environment filled with certainty and signs of progress. Decisive leaders are key for an atmosphere of success.

Decisiveness does not imply we must possess all of the knowledge to reach a verdict, either. A wise leader taps into the creativity of his followers. He allows their hands-on experience to guide his decisions. This applies to our personal lives as well. A husband may be the ultimate decision-maker in the family, but he relies on the input of his wife and values her opinion. The fact that we do not have to know everything should be a big confidence booster! We can safely turn to others for assistance.

The support and confidence of those around us is gained when they believe we place their welfare first. A self-serving leader will quickly lose respect. Followers will not trust someone who doesn't have their best interests at heart. They will feel used and betrayed. We must remember to place the group's welfare and success above all else if we are to earn confidence and loyalty.

OVERCOMING

"Successful leaders know when to back away and let others take the credit."
- Bill Myers, Columbus (OH) Health Commissioner,
1980-2002

OBSTACLES

Just as the leader lacks confidence without sufficient information, so do his followers. They will falter and veer off course without proper instruction and guidance. Be precise with requests and let people know what is expected of them. If subordinates have to guess what we want, their uncertainty will result in poor decisions and unproductive behavior. Keep others properly informed and aware of expectations.

Confidence and organization affect every aspect of a group, from the leaders to the followers. These skills can be learned and are vital to our success. If we want to overcome our fears and achieve our goals, we must develop these qualities. It can mean the difference between a potential leader and a dynamic leader!

In a nutshell...
- Organization and confidence inspires followers
- Knowledge and structure give us confidence
- Form a plan and take steps to organize
- Confidence leads to decisiveness
- Followers need confidence and organization as well

29

Never Take Criticism Personally

When we stick our heads above the crowd, we invite criticism. Leaders in particular are vulnerable as their movement is always under scrutiny. After all, it's not about winning a popularity contest; it's about doing the right thing. If we are to persevere, we cannot fear criticism or judgment.

Several reasons exist for criticism. Humans fear what they do not understand. They fear anything that is not deemed normal. When witnessing another person attempting something new, some respond with negative criticism. They might also feel envy or jealousy. The individual in pursuit of his goal is taking away all excuses. Sometimes a critic simply possesses a different viewpoint. He may be just casually expressing this fact or totally refusing to see the matter in another light. Then there are those who love to criticize because they feel it is their duty!

The best protection against criticism is to avoid taking it personally. Many times the judgment is not aimed directly at us, but we accept it as such. If our egos were not on the line, we would not feel so threatened! By removing our self-esteems from the equation, we find that criticism does little harm. We are then better equipped to handle criticism calmly and effectively.

Author and Pastor, Bill Wilson, has this to say about taking criticism personally:

Six reasons why you shouldn't take criticism personally:

1. You'll develop a martyr's complex. A martyr spends too much time thinking of himself.
2. Taking criticism personally causes us to isolate ourselves from others.
3. Taking criticism personally means we'll suffer without the support of others.
4. When a person is secure in himself, he won't take an insult personally.
5. If you don't take a criticism personally, you won't feel the need to retaliate personally.
6. When you take something personally, you give another person control of your emotions. E.g.: Actress Julia Roberts- A commentator said she was the worst dressed woman at the Oscars. She said she was depressed for two weeks.

- Bill Wilson, author & Pastor of The Lord's Table

As is evidenced by the reasons for criticism, it is often a fearful or angry response and tends to elicit a similar reaction in us. We feel threatened by the negative attack, even if the criticism was not aimed at us directly. Our self-preservation instincts are strong, and we are inclined to defend our position. Reacting out of anger does not always help our position, though. Often this will only encourage the critic to pursue the issue further. Human nature dictates that he will fight back if cornered and may even welcome a verbal brawl! We set ourselves up for a long battle if we choose to respond negatively to the critic's words or actions.

OVERCOMING

"My view is that if it is about you then, actually, it is personal. Accepting it is the key. If you sulk, people will move away from you and not approach again, thus limiting your own growth."
- Dirk Robertson BSc (Hons) CQSW, FCE, Writer, Chair of The London School of Economics Alumni Mentoring Committee www.dirkrobertson.com

Contrary to our desires, we do not need to respond to every criticism. We are better served if we pick and choose our battles wisely! Most negative comments do not even warrant a response. Only when it damages principles, especially those of our group or organization, should we step up and defend ourselves. In general, though, it is simply best to ignore the criticism. If our reputation is solid and we are not at fault, then the truth will usually prevail.

Despite our efforts to remain neutral, sometimes criticism gets the best of us and we feel angry and resentful. Rather than lash out at our apparent nemesis and begin an ugly war of words, we need to consider this trick. Drain negative emotions by writing a letter to that individual or organization. Do not hold back feelings, either. Pour all frustrations onto that sheet of paper. When finished with this masterpiece of bitter retort, reread it and make sure all of the points have been covered. Once satisfied that no issue remains unsaid, destroy this letter! Under no condition should it be sent to the recipient. The objective is to drain our negative feelings without damaging the other person.

Occasionally we can employ a little humor to diffuse the situation. We can respond with a comeback so outlandish that no one will even remember the original criticism. Perhaps we can offer a comedic but true observation in regards to our critic. A minor embarrassment with no viable rejoinder at his disposal will certainly silence the individual! Of course, if there is any truth to the matter, we may need to apply humor to ourselves. The man who can laugh at criticisms of himself will earn more respect that the one who returns punches.

Criticism may also come down to one simple fact. We were wrong. Unfortunately, leadership does not imply that we are always correct. No one enjoys admitting a mistake, but sometimes that is our only option. We must own up to our errors and willingly offer to correct the situation. A person with a weak or frail self-image will struggle with this action. However, if our self-esteem resides in the positive and we have not placed our ego on the line, then admitting we are wrong will not devastate us. We will be viewed in a better light if we are honest and forthcoming.

Ultimately, does the criticism really matter? Sometimes we must take the 'who cares?' attitude. If it is just one opinion out of millions, it does not hold a great deal of weight. Treat the response as if conducting a survey- drop the top and bottom answers. Do not waste time and energy on an extreme judgment.

We will face critics at every corner, even more so when we pursue worthwhile goals. Be prepared for criticism and remove personal consideration from the equation. Negative judgment cannot harm us if we refuse to take it personal. Criticism is one fear we don't want to take with us on the road to success!

In a nutshell...
1. There are several reasons for criticism
2. We may feel threatened and desire to retaliate
3. Best defense is to avoid taking criticism personally
4. Not all criticism deserves a response
5. Employ humor to handle the situation

30

Invite Ideas to Keep Moving

Ideas and input from others can help us overcome fears and reach goals. In this world, true success is rarely achieved alone! Assistance is vital if we want to keep moving forward and achieve our dreams.

There's a saying, 'If it's not broke, don't fix it', but sometimes change is necessary. People and businesses alike find themselves in a rut if they don't continue growing and transforming. Progress cannot be made while standing still. We must innovate and encourage change.

If we are not encountering the desired results, then change is our only option. Practices and tactics that worked in the past may not apply to current situations. We should not simply resign ourselves to old patterns and procedures if the outcome is unfavorable. Stupidity is repeating an action and expecting different results! Whether it involves business or personal, we must break away from unfruitful practices and stale systems and innovate a new approach.

"Effective leaders not only embrace change, they create it."
- Bill Myers, Columbus (OH) Health Commissioner,
1980-2002

Nothing stimulates growth quite like the pooling of resources and ideas. Soliciting suggestions from others should not be feared but embraced. The leader doesn't always know the details of the daily grind. Our followers are even closer to the issue and undoubtedly possess worthwhile solutions. Occasionally the leader needs to look to the leader over him, as that person may have faced similar problems. This line of thought applies to personal challenges as well. Those who have successfully traveled the road before us can offer valuable information and suggestions.

This does not mean we have to act upon or accept every recommendation. Every person has an opinion, but not every opinion carries merit. Sift through the ideas and advice, discarding what cannot be used, and focus only on the valid points. The fresh viewpoints will stir our imagination and cause the creative juices to flow. Often we discover a suggestion that in turn sparks a similar but better idea in our minds. By reaching out for assistance, we may find the perfect solution!

Those in a leadership position need to turn to their subordinates for help. Put those dull, weekly meetings to use! Ask for suggestions and allow everyone the opportunity to speak. At first, ideas will be slow in coming as followers attempt to gauge the sincerity of the leader. Keep encouraging contributions. If someone offers a worthy suggestion and it is put to use, be sure that individual receives credit, too.

The benefits of such practice are numerous. We let our followers know that we value their efforts, respect their opinions, and will acknowledge their contributions. We feed their egos and gain their respect and trust. And, we achieve our original objective-we receive a solution to our problem.

Once we open the door to suggestions, though, we cannot slam it shut on people's toes. If someone's idea does not work, condemning that individual will cause hard feelings and stifle further input. When others fear punishment for failure, the flow of ideas will abruptly cease. The ultimate decision was ours, and there the blame should rest as well. We need to keep channels open if we hope to continue receiving assistance.

What if someone offers a better idea than our own? We must be prepared for this to happen! If our self-esteem is low, we'll feel unreceptive to suggestions and threatened by other's solutions. In such a situation, we have to decide if we want to be right or if we want our problems solved. Our ego may have to take a back seat! This is why it is vital that we maintain a positive self-image. When we are secure with ourselves, we will be more open to ideas and suggestions from others.

At this point, one might wonder why a chapter on inviting ideas resides in the overcoming fear section. Simply phrased, when there is no apparent solution, obstacles and problems cause fear. By inviting ideas, we increase our chances of overcoming these difficulties and eliminating the fear. No potential resource should go untapped!

Once we have selected a destination, we should never waver in our decision to reach that objective. Problems will arise, and we will make mistakes. The secret is to learn from these experiences. The law of averages says if we keep trying, if we are persistent and consistent, eventually we will succeed. Thomas Edison and his ten thousand attempts to create the light bulb should give us hope! It is doubtful we will encounter that many unsuccessful endeavors as we move toward our goal. However, we must be willing to do whatever it takes to conquer fear and achieve success.

Sometimes it requires drastic and desperate measures to keep us moving forward. If we find we've hit the wall and exhausted every known resource, the only option may be to burn the boats. This expression comes from an old tale. An army once landed on an island, and upon discovering an even greater army in residence, the soldiers were afraid to fight. Their leader solved the problem by burning their boats, thus giving them no other option but to fight! (Not surprisingly, they defeated the army present on the island.)

The army found their motivation when confronted with no escape. What boats do we need to burn that would motivate us to continue moving forward?

There is always a solution to any problem. Seek assistance and suggestions from others before admitting defeat. Success is always closer than we think. And if all else fails, burn the boats!

In a nutshell...
- We must encourage and accept change
- Solicit suggestions from others
- Keep channels open for ideas

- Someone else's recommendation may be better
- Law of averages says we'll succeed eventually
- Sometimes we must burn the boats

Key 5

Setting Goals

Goals are what give us purpose in life. Equipped with a target and a plan, our existence holds meaning. Without dreams and aspirations, we simply drift through this world like a leaf on a river.

Many times our dreams become lost in the daily shuffle. We must redefine our goals and keep them in front of us at all times. Armed with a vision, we can accomplish anything in this world.

Which leads us to the final Key- setting goals!

31

Living With a Purpose

Goals are empowering. They give us the strength to persevere even through the most difficult situations. Our lives are enriched when we live with a purpose!

Possessing a goal provides a person with something for which to strive. He has a target and destiny awaiting his arrival. Goals give our lives meaning and a reason to continue moving forward. The man with something to live for lives longer! Therefore, we need to set goals, if only to live a long and productive life.

Master Chaplain, Bob Johnson, has this to say about living life with a purpose:

When I found out that I had a purpose, it changed my perspective of life. It gave me new meaning. Realizing that life had more to it than just work or play gave me a zeal I didn't know I had. It opened new doors to my mind that drives me to this day. I love the fact that having a purpose gives me a new day everyday. I get up feeling energized and confident that something new is going to happen. Now that's exciting!

With this new thought of purpose, I can set goals. When I awake in the morning knowing I have a reason for living; my goal that day is to accomplish whatever I need to do so life is filled with a joy that touches lives and helps me to see things in a different way. My steps become more brisk, my smile becomes wider and more real. So many people smile but don't mean it. It's just a cover up for what's hurting inside. Just the other day my wife said to me, "When I smile, it hurts, so when I smile for others, it's just fake." I thought about that statement and it hit home. We do cover up our true feelings. I believe when we fail to set honest goals about our life we have a tendency to cover up our feelings. It would do us good to overcome our hurts by seeking to do good deeds for others. This has a mental and physical response on our bodies. In other words, it makes us feel good.

When we set goals remember to set realistic ones. Ones we can obtain easily and ones we have to work harder at so we can have a challenge. Also remember, goals are for fun as well. Without fun and laughter, our life would fade into a dull, dark place. Laughter is good medicine.

As I get older, I am finding that the more I dream, the more things happen. I want to try new things and start new adventures. This becomes energizing and exciting. I am about to retire from one job, and I am looking forward to new adventures. Knowing this sparks my mind, which I believe, moves my body to want to live longer. Having a purpose gives me the knowledge that life can be fulfilling and drives me to want to have life and have it more abundantly. Don't be afraid to change. Change can be a good thing. It can help our desires become more exciting. It gives us new perspectives about our goals. It becomes burned into our hearts and minds and allows us to grow. Don't let fear of change become a stumbling block to your life and your purpose. Allow purpose to open doors to a more invigorating life.

When you're at a stopping place, take a moment to write down your ideas and goals. Take time to make a list of the dreams you have; list the goals to achieve these dreams and give yourself permission to act on them. Visualizing these helps them to become more a part of your mind and heart. It gives you a place to go to see how you are doing. I have done this, and when I see I have accomplished a goal, it energizes me to continue on my trek to greater things. If I haven't yet reached my goal, it gives me the latitude to write other ideas down so I can reach it or change directions. Do you have a burning desire to accomplish a dream? Go for it. Take the step in faith and see where it leads. In Jeremiah 29:11 it says "'I know the plans I have for you,' says the Lord. 'Plans for your welfare and not your harm, to give you and future and hope.'" These words have motivated me to keep on dreaming and hoping that the purpose God has for me will be completed.

- Master Chaplain, Bob Johnson, ATF chaplain, US Marshall Chaplain, Law Enforcement chaplain, lifetime member of the ICPC, former FBI chaplain, Disaster team and peer support team member, author, teacher, motivational speaker & presenter www.bobjohnsonministries.com

Goals are obviously not reserved just for youth! We can set goals at any stage in our life. There are no limitations except those we place on ourselves.

To ensure the goal-setting process is truly effective, we must set short, mid-range, and long-range goals. Success is built on many small steps, and before we can hit the primary target, we must reach smaller targets first. Once we have determined the finish line, we can set daily, weekly, and monthly goals that will keep us on track. These smaller goals not only keep us progressing toward our desired destination, they build confidence as we achieve small successes along the way.

First, we need to select our main ambition. What do we really want in life? What hopes and dreams have yet to see fruition? If it's been a long time since we truly set a goal, we may need to do some soul-searching. Dig deep and recall the dreams of youth. When we were young, we did not possess the inhibitions and limitations that we experience as adults. We may need to rekindle the fire of those memories and brush the dust off our early aspirations. Write down every desire and dream that comes to mind, no matter how incredible.

Once we have a comprehensive list, we need to carefully consider each item. Which goals are simply wants? These are things that would be nice but not necessary. Which items are needs? These are the goals that must happen or are essential to our fulfillment as a person. Separate the list into these two categories. Focus on personal desire, not what others might feel is important. These are our dreams and belong to us, so our opinion is the one that matters.

Now, which of the needs is a burning desire? As we say in the South, which goal is a 'gots to have'? It must be an aspiration that excites us and inspires enthusiasm. Which need best fits that description? This is the goal that will cause us to move mountains and do whatever it takes to accomplish. Resist the urge to select a safe goal, though. Plausibility will not matter if it's not a passionate desire!

OVERCOMING

"We all have dreams, but if you want them to come true you have to have goals. A goal is a dream with a plan and a deadline. It becomes real and tangible when you write it down. Then set interim goals, small successes that will lead to your big success. Look at your plan every day so your purpose is always in your mind. And remember to be like a turtle. Not just because slow and steady wins the race, but also because the turtle only makes progress when he sticks his neck out."
- Austin S. Camacho, author of the Hannibal Jones Mysteries
www.ascamacho.com

OBSTACLES

We can set goals all day long, but until we make the decision to pursue them, nothing happens. Make the decision to achieve these goals! Resolution flicks a switch in our brains and immediately our minds go to work plotting a path. The dream must precede the planning stage or there will not be enough reason for us to form a plan. We must also view this goal every day. Write it down and place in a prominent place. Written goals are more likely to be accomplished than ones residing in our thoughts alone. We must be reminded every day of our decision!

Living with a purpose means we live life to the fullest. Personal satisfaction and enrichment awaits those who decide to pursue a dream. Select a goal today. Equipped with a passionate vision, we can achieve anything!

In a nutshell...
- Goals give our life purpose and meaning
- Pursuing dreams excites and inspires us
- Visualize where you want to go
- Set short, mid, and long-range goals
- Determine your burning desire
- Make the decision to pursue your passion

32

Starting on the Path

Whenever we attempt something new in life, the first step is always the most difficult. We know where to go but not how to reach that destination! Forming a plan is essential to success, and we need to maintain the right attitude in the process, too.

The decision is essentially the first step. As previously stated, that sends our brains into action. The subconscious goes to work formulating a strategy. Now that we are focused on a target, circumstances begin to change. We see opportunities that did not exist previously. Ideas will hit us in the middle of the night. Begin to write down every inspiration, no matter how far-fetched. This is the beginning stage of organizing a plan.

OVERCOMING

"The best ideas I've seen in life aren't complicated. They are based primarily on fundamental logic and easily understood by a majority of people. A creative idea, then, that is also a sound idea, can be life-changing in personal lives and in the life of a business. Once an individual or company is satisfied that the idea is feasible, then comes the greatest challenge: can you execute it effectively?"
- Robert Rehder, Dean of College Advancement,
James Sprunt Community College

As plausible ideas emerge, map out several potential strategies. Select the most concise plan on which to focus energy. Organize and solidify this course of action and remember to leave open all options. As they say, nothing ever goes according to plan, so leave room for contingencies. Do not lose sight of the goal during this stage, either! Concentrate on the final destination, not all of the potential problems in between.

The initial planning process should not be excessively long. Even if we are planning a monumental step, such as starting a business, we still need to move toward the goal, if only to continue acquiring information. How can we properly plan if do not possess all the facts? We certainly cannot prepare for every situation that may or may not arise! It will require action to formulate a complete strategy. Start taking the first few steps, gathering information and momentum in the process.

Remember to watch the words pouring from mind and lips! Remain positive and optimistic in all areas. Avoid the words *if*, *maybe*, and *whenever*. They are negative and self-defeating. We want our brains dwelling on victory not failure. Instead, speak as if success has already been achieved. This reinforces the mind's determination to make our vision a reality.

Master Chaplain, Bob Johnson, shares his thoughts on the path to success:

These words from Jeremiah have given me the direction I have needed. The path to reaching your goal or dream is not to worry. Worry is a detriment to any path you might want to take. It will stop you in your tracks. You become anxious over any movement you might want to take. Your thoughts become jumbled and thinking becomes impossible. Worry takes desire away. You become tired more easily, and when you want to try something new, fear sets in. It drives you backwards, to retreat, to hide from the possible and guides you into the impossible. Worry stops you from making decisions so you can't pursue your goal. You become indecisive which puts us into a world of confusion. Life becomes filled with false thoughts and keeps us from acting on our desires.

So, what do we do? Simple, allow ourselves to fall back on our faith in God and ourselves. You see, nothing is impossible with God in control. Faith and trust moves us forward and allows us to breathe a breath of clean air. It lets us take stock of who we belong to and that our gifts are from above. You see, He wants us to use our gifts so others can benefit from our dreams and goals. Now, that's powerful. Just knowing we are making a difference can give us a joy that satisfies the soul.

Another thought that comes to mind is to think and act positively. Negative thoughts keep us defensive. It takes away the good attitude and instills in us a barrier to any further thoughts that will help us accomplish our goals. God doesn't think negatively nor should we. God believes in us. That should give us hope to go forward with positive results.

There is a word that comes to mind. The word is persistence. In other words, don't quit. Don't give up. Keep on striving to reach your dream or goal. Push until it hurts. I assure you, by doing all you can to reach your goal and being persistent in your attitude, you will grow and finally reach the goal or start a new one. You see, it's not the destination; it's the journey. To make that destination worthwhile and the journey fun, persistence is the answer. Being positive is the cure. Discipline yourself to do both, and you will obtain your goals and your pathway will be successful.

- Master Chaplain, Bob Johnson, ATF chaplain, US Marshall Chaplain, Law Enforcement chaplain, lifetime member of the ICPC, former FBI chaplain, Disaster team and peer support team member, author, teacher, motivational speaker & presenter www.bobjohnsonministries.com

A burning desire requires daily effort to maintain. We need to be consistent and persistent in our endeavors. Infrequent and inconsistent action results in a weakening of the dream's power to motivate us. We lose sight of the goal. Perseverance and consistency is required if we ever hope to succeed. An occasional drop of water will not wear away a stone, but a constant trickle will eventually erode the surface. We must apply this persistence when pursuing our dreams and goals.

This steadfast attitude requires discipline. There will be days when we do not feel like pursuing our ambitions. Exhaustion, apathy, and time constraints will wear on our resolution. When these moments occur, only discipline will keep pushing us forward. Our enthusiasm might wane, but this internal training of self-control will prevent us from faltering off course.

 OVERCOMING

"Set a timeline. Believe in yourself. Make it happen. Be proud of what you accomplish."
- Lynn Tincher, author of Afterthoughts
www.lynntincher.com

 OBSTACLES

Every aspect of pursuing a goal needs to become a habit. The process itself should be part of our daily routine and as automatic as brushing our teeth. Chasing a dream invites new experiences, but there's always reoccurring details involved. By setting daily goals to accomplish these tasks, we train ourselves to instinctively perform these duties. Habits traditionally take twenty-one days to form. During those three weeks, it is critical we establish patterns. When we grow weary, it will be these habits that ensure our continued pursuit of our goals.

Life's journeys were meant to be shared. Seek the support of a trusted and reliable individual. He can offer encouragement when we experience setbacks, prodding us to continue forward. Perhaps this person is pursuing a similar goal, such as losing weight, and will provide us with a measure of accountability. Our confidant could be a mentor who can guide us over the rough patches. Regardless of this person's identity, we all tend to perform better with a cheerleader in our corner. When faced with challenges and obstacles blocking the path to our goal, we need every possible encouragement!

The road may appear long, but it will grow shorter with every step. Formulate a plan and start reducing the expanse by taking action.

In a nutshell...
- Be open to new ideas as they emerge
- Begin to formulate a plan of action
- Take any action to get the ball rolling
- Avoid negative feelings and thoughts

OVERCOMING OBSTACLES WITH SPUNK!

- Develop persistence, consistence, and discipline
- Seek support and encouragement from a friend

33

Develop Vision with Passion

Goals survive and flourish on passion and determination. Those possessing a vision must act with enthusiasm and belief. Organizations thrive when the leader is able to embody its vision. If we are to see our individual dreams come true, we need to exhibit our vision as well.

Author Darlene Ford Wofford shares her experience:

Don't "buy into" the negative!
Success is relative from one individual to another. One person defines success as a life of abundance, good health, a loving family, and the ability to provide a roof over their heads and food on the table. Another is driven by money, career, and material things. Then there are those who define it as "having it all"- spirituality, good health, loving family, position, material things, and the security of financial freedom.

Many set goals but are not *goal-driven*, thus "success" is usually not in their vocabulary or life experiences, and most likely, the same applies among their immediate circle. "Like attracts like." "Birds of a feather flock together." "Winners run with winners." So, if you're aspiring to win in life, assess your "flock" of friends and associates. If conversations include dreams and goals, with accomplishments encouraged and lauded, you're likely flying with the eagles, and more apt to ascend to heights of achievement. Conversely, if they're defined by negative attitudes and "downer" topics such as money problems, ill-fated relationships, and poor health, etc., you'll be less likely to get off the ground. It's difficult to gain momentum in order to reach the altitude required to realize aspirations when weighted down with the woes of the world. Among the "downer" group are pessimists, "nay-sayers," and saboteurs casting doubt and discouragement, as it seems their favorite response is "that will never happen," or "that won't work." Unintentional as it may be on their part, your balloon is often burst by their negative reactions. Don't buy into them- they simply don't share your optimism and vision. Jealousy often prevents them from supporting you, or they fear you will outgrow them and move on to another group of friends when you're successful. Case in point: Exercise caution when it comes to those with whom you share your goals, and don't "buy into" the negative!

Bottom line: success comes to those who set goals and strive to achieve them.

Daily goals met lead to yearly goals met,
And so on and so on it goes.
It's the wise that set new goals as others are met,
For a time without goals leads to a time of regret.
- Darlene Ford Wofford- July 30, 1985

Passion Outshines Ominous Forecasts

October 4, 1985, I was in an automobile accident sustaining multiple injuries, the most critical to my right leg. An extensive surgery was performed, implanting enough metal in my leg to set off any airport detector; however, there was no guarantee I would ever walk again. I was confined to a wheel chair for a year, slowly progressing to a walker, and later crutches. Three years and four surgeries later, I was thrilled to walk again, even if I had to do so wearing a three-pound leg brace and using a cane.

July 1988, the doctors' prognoses concurred I would never walk without the brace and cane. *"Why me?"* was my foremost thought as I threw myself a huge pity-party and included anyone who would listen. I was mad at the driver of the other car, and mad at my doctors for not putting "Humpty Dumpty" back together again.

A few weeks later, my mother became ill and hospitalized. I loved her more than life itself. I kept remembering how often she expressed nothing would make her happier than seeing me walk again without the brace and cane. At her age of 78 and failing health, it looked doubtful that would happen.

But what could I do about it? After all, the doctors said... Suddenly I recalled my mother's words, "Dahleen, you can do ANYTHING you set your mind to." I knew she was right as I thought, *I CAN do this! The doctors just don't know whom they're dealing with!* I couldn't envision myself crippled for the rest of my life. I refused to buy into the doctors' ominous forecasts for my future.

I then envisioned walking for my mother, and I declared the goal to do so with one primary purpose- to bring a smile to my mother's face. It was no longer all about ME, but about bringing joy to another. The goal of walking became my project. The more I envisioned walking again with the overall purpose of making my mother happy, the more passionate I became about my project. As my leg gained strength, I saw myself walking without so much as a limp. At least that was how I envisioned myself upon waking in the morning and when I closed my eyes every night. However, I took caution in sharing my goal with those who might express skepticism- I couldn't afford to bring doubt into the equation.

My vision became reality as I met my goal October 12, 1988- my 40th birthday. Mother died the following spring, but she died having seen me walk again, and I'll always have the beautiful memory of her smiling face. By my 41st birthday, I was indeed walking without so much as a limp, as I danced in the arms of my husband.

Whenever passion-felt purpose is assigned to a project,
the more passionate one becomes about the project.
As passion accelerates, the project excels.
Vision- Seeing is Believing!

Medical science reveals the visual part of the human brain is three times the size of the remainder. That's the reason we believe what we see. Seeing *is* believing!

I've been familiar with the *Vision* or *Dream Board* for years, however never "took the time" to create one. In September 2007, I was compelled to do so. I worked on it steadily until 3:00 that afternoon. I cut out magazine pictures that best represented my wildest dreams and visions for my life. I divided my board into two parts- Professional and Personal. On the Personal side, I placed the words "Loving Relationships" in bold letters along with photos of my family and friends. I included an airplane and cruise ship, as well as beach and mountain scenes, representing travel and places my husband and I look forward to visiting.

On the Professional side went pictures and words like "Success," "Follow Your Passion," "Motivate," "Inspire," "Wealth, Good Health & Happiness," all relating to my career as an image consultant, speaker & author. There's a close-up of a happy-faced, smiling, successful-looking woman wearing a fur coat in a red convertible, and a full-length shot of a hot little red convertible. *(I now own a hot little red Thunderbird convertible).* I wanted to expand my speaking engagements so I placed a photo of a nice meeting room set up for such an event. *(I have since spoken before many groups in similar beautiful settings).* I've always wanted to be a featured speaker at a resort- complimentary massages included- so I added a picture of a woman getting a massage. *(About 6:00 that evening, I received a call from the coordinator for a women's retreat at a wonderful resort in the North Georgia Mountains. She invited me to speak at the next retreat that January!)* When she added how incredible their massages are, I remember thinking, *Wow, this thing really works fast!*

Compelled to finish the Board, I included logos for television channels and photos of talk show hosts. *(In 2008, I was contacted by two of the talk shows and featured on TV.)* I placed a mock flyer with the words "Award-Winning Author" preceding my name. *(In January '08 an international book contest notified me that my book won "Best Autobiography" and I was recognized "Author of the Year" for 2007).* I also placed pictures of the actress I would like to see depict the protagonist in a movie based on my novel, *Edgewise: An Assignment to Remember. (A film production company is considering a movie project based on the story).* Last but certainly not least, I included the logo for Children's Healthcare of Atlanta because we direct a portion of the proceeds to them in memory of our son. I've learned that whenever I assign a purpose to any project I undertake, my passion for the project accelerates- and as my passion accelerates, I excel at the project. My Vision Board has a prominent place in my office so I see it every day. I continue to add to it, and as it is filled, I will begin another one.

Imagining your unlimited possibilities, then bringing them to life on the Vision Board ultimately leads to living your wildest dreams. *Seeing truly IS believing!*

To create your very own Vision Board you will need the following:
- · White Poster Board
- · Magazines
- · Scissors
- · Glue Stick or Paste
- · Colored Marker (optional)
- · Imagination/ Open Mind filled with Visions and Dreams for Your Future (mandatory)

Fill Your Nights with Dreams of Discovery...
Fulfill Your Days with the Fascinations of Exploring.
- Darlene Ford Wofford- January, 1984,
©The Spirited Southerner www.SpiritedSoutherner.com

If we act with conviction, others will follow our vision, too. Our passion must be real and felt from the heart. Believe in your vision and see it clearly, and then watch your dreams come to life!

In a nutshell...
- • To achieve goals, we must be goal-driven
- • Associate with winners
- • Believe that you CAN
- • We must truly see our vision
- • Create your own Dream Board

34

Take Charge, Take Action

The achievement of goals is not a passive occurrence. Action is required. Change is necessary. Our attitude needs adjusting. We cannot sit back and wait for circumstances and events to align perfectly. We need to take the bull by the horns and actively pursue our dreams.

Growth and maturity dictate that we take responsibility for ourselves. Regardless of our age, we need to be accountable for our actions and thoughts. We must accept the blame as well as the credit. Leaders realize they must shoulder the responsibility of their behavior and decisions. Playing the victim card only empowers problems. It does not solve these challenges or provide strength. On the contrary, victims are helpless and not in control of their destiny. Refuse to surrender to outside forces and other people! We can only discover answers and solutions when we accept responsibility for our lives.

By refusing to accept the role of victim, we are less likely to fixate on the past. We should learn from our mistakes without obsessing over errors and lost opportunities. Lamenting 'if only' does nothing for our current situation. Yes, our circumstances and the surrounding issues might be different 'if only'. Get over it and move forward! We cannot change the past, only the present and future. Take what was learned and focus on the tasks ahead.

The best analogy is to consider our life as an open book. We all begin with blank pages that slowly fill as time passes. However, fate is not writing this story- we are creating the tale. Each day is a fresh page and we fill it with our choices, actions and words. Once written, it cannot be changed. We can't go back and erase previous pages. Neither can we leaf forward and write on those pages. We only have today, and each morning, we start anew. What was written previously in our book holds no real power over us. We should feel relieved and excited by this fact! Every day is a fresh beginning and a new direction in our life.

Great leaders realize that despite the best of intentions, they will make mistakes. All they can do is correct the situation, improving on the present while building for the future. However, mistakes are not the only thing that should remain in the past. Our thoughts should not be filled with past accomplishments, either. We need to recall these moments of triumph, as they will spur us to more success. It's when they consume our thoughts to the point of obsession that it becomes a problem. Basking in past glory prevents us from moving forward and eliminates the possibility of further achievements. If we wait for a reward, hoping the accomplishment will garner praise for our leadership skills, we may find ourselves waiting for a very long time!

Do not let achievement induce a false sense of security. We cannot rest on our laurels, expecting to enjoy the attention and glory indefinitely. We will not accomplish anything under those conditions. Eventually we will lose sight of our dream and cease to grow and change. We'll join the ranks of those who talk a good game but refuse to take action or perhaps slip into old, negative habits. Caught in stagnation, we may resort to accusations and grumbling, offering a variety of reasons why we are not moving forward. (And complainers contribute little to any group!) Turn the page and begin working on a new chapter.

Occasionally a major event will spark our desire to change and set goals. We may experience a life-changing incident that prompts reevaluation. A spiritual or emotional revolution might spur transformation. In the case of an alcoholic or drug user, drastic changes will be necessary if that individual wants to alter his future. He's got a lot of bad habits to erase!

However, most of us do not need to radically revamp our world. An exciting new dream might inspire us to instigate many changes in hopes of attaining this goal. Adjustments will indeed be necessary as we alter our path and cast aside distractions and obstacles. Trouble arises when we attempt to change everything at once and then feel overwhelmed by the scope of such a transformation. Sooner or later, we feel tempted to quit. Remember to take small steps and build on these minor victories and changes. Make small adjustments and work gradually toward the goal rather than attempt one giant leap.

OVERCOMING

"Don't set your goal so big that it is unrealistic. Even if you sincerely believe that EVERYONE needs to know and understand the product or expertise that you have to offer, you cannot possibly get your message to everyone. Carve out a more manageable niche to which you can market your products and services. You will make more of an impact if you concentrate on those potential customers who have a need they recognize for what you have to offer. Spend your funds and energies going strongly after that niche market instead of having a scattergun approach that dissipates your efforts."
- Judith C. Hoffman, Principal, JCH Enterprises Community and Media Relations, Author of "Keeping Cool on the Hot Seat: Dealing Effectively with the Media in Times of Crisis"
www.judyhoffman.com

At the end of every day, analyze all results. If we have missed the mark, make adjustments and try again tomorrow. If the plan failed, adjust and attempt a new course of action. Occasionally a plan takes time, but if the strategy is not working, stubbornly refusing to change will not accomplish the task. Remember, placing our ego on the line only invites discouragement. Accept that there will be mistakes, without allowing this fact to destroy the self-image, and get excited by the prospect! With every mistake and subsequent adjustment, we move closer to the goal- and ultimately success.

We are responsible for writing our life's story. Refuse to dwell in the past, as those pages have long since been turned. Focus on what can be controlled and changed. Accept the challenge to create a successful tomorrow by taking charge today!

In a nutshell...
- Take responsibility for the future
- Do not live in the glory of past success
- We must continue to move forward
- Radical change is not always necessary
- Make adjustments as needed

35

Making it All Work

The journey toward our goals can appear quite overwhelming at times! We struggle with the best approach, fight to continue moving forward, and feel frustrated when things go wrong. This is why short-term goals and a simple method for organizing are so important. They act as building blocks and keep us on the path.

Author and good friend, p.m. terrell, has come up with a unique method to tackle these problems:

"Lego™ Writing"

After running two corporations for 18 years, I decided to opt for semi-retirement and begin a full-time writing career. I had worked on a number of projects ranging from hour-long to multi-year commitments; but when I started my writing career, I realized there was nothing quite as daunting as staring at a blank computer screen and knowing I must write a 300-page book in six months. The plot has never been a difficult thing for me to envision. I write suspense/thrillers and being a conspiracy theorist at heart; I find plot ideas everywhere I look. It's taking a monumental task and breaking it down into something manageable, something that doesn't seem as overwhelming, that is often difficult to mentally break through.

With one book due to the publisher each year, I know I don't have the luxury of procrastination, just as people in the corporate world must meet their deadlines. For me, one missed deadline affects a dozen people in the production chain; and since my publisher releases books only in the spring and fall, a missed deadline could mean a delay of six to twelve months. That, in turn, greatly affects my financial situation.

I've learned a system to tackling a huge job, a system I call Lego™ Work.

We all remember Legos™ as a child, those toy building blocks that allowed us to create almost anything our imaginations could conjure: houses, castles, cities, even vehicles. And yet every creation began with two blocks set side by side or atop of one another. Then one more building block, followed by another. And another and another, until we had a basic structure. That structure then became larger and more elaborate until our final creation was complete.

In Lego™ Work, I envision my final goal: in my case, it is a completed book with approximately 100,000 polished words between the covers; a complex story with interesting characters and a compelling plot woven through subplots like a fine tapestry.

Next, I look at my time frame. Six months from the date I have agreed to begin, the book must be finished and sent to the editors. That leaves me with roughly 26 weeks. A little bit of division tells me I must write just under 4,000 words each week to meet this goal.

Realistically, I can count on writing four days a week. That means each day I write, I must aim for 1,000 words.

So, with Lego™ Work, I envision the final result and then break it down into monthly, weekly, and daily goals.

When I first began writing, I tried to make every sentence, every paragraph, every page the best I could write- in the first draft. With ten books behind me and many more in front, I've come to realize that editing is much easier once the words are on paper. I needn't think of whether my writing is relevant to the plot; I simply need to get those words on paper.

It's just like building a house. There will always be unexpected turns- a change in the work order, something that doesn't quite fit, something else that needs to be reworked. But if you plan for those changes, if you anticipate them, you won't be thrown off-course when they come at you.

When you think about those hours in which you built that house or castle or city with building blocks, you'll remember how focused you were. Time stood still. Focus is everything. With my writing project, I go back over it and massage it, making sure all of the elements are in place- what the characters are seeing, feeling, smelling, hearing, touching. I become so engrossed in what I am building that by the time I reach that last word, I am ready for the next one.

But I don't try to write it.

Instead, I type notes on the next page, notes that remind me what I want to write the following day. Sometimes, they are cryptic and brief; other times, they are wordy and filled with description.

Then I leave those thoughts to cook in my brain, to gel and come together. I live with the next scene. As I lay in bed before sleep comes, I envision the people, the events, and all those emotions and activities that come along with the next chapter. I am building in my mind, the same way an architect does when envisioning his or her next project. I am creating the blueprint in my mind's eye.

When my father worked for the FBI, he said each evening before the agents left work they were expected to complete index cards for the next day's assignments. He learned this process relieved a lot of stress and they hit the ground running the next day because their assignments and goals had already been planned.

Similarly, with each day that passes, my Lego™ Work is built, one sentence, one paragraph, one page, one chapter at a time. And before I know it, I have 1,000, 10,000 and then 50,000 words. In six months, I have a manuscript I can send to the editors. I have completed my project, one Lego™ at a time.

- p.m. terrell, author, speaker, & co-founder of The Book 'Em Foundation www.pmterrell.com, www.bookemfoundation.org, and www.maryneely.com

We often make the process more difficult that necessary. Learn to simplify. Make use of building blocks. Tackle dreams and goals as one would eat an elephant- one bite at a time!

In a nutshell...
- Do not feel overwhelmed by the task
- Break it down into manageable steps
- Set smaller daily & weekly goals
- Do not aim for perfection
- Plan for the next day's goals

36

When the Goal Becomes Fuzzy

There will be moments during our quest when the goal loses clarity. Obstacles will loom on every side, critics will condemn our attempts, and those following our lead will question our decisions. What appeared so clear when we first began grows fuzzy, and we wonder if we'll ever reach our destination. Why does this happen and how do we correct the situation?

When we first set a goal, our eyes are focused on the target. All attention and energy converges on reaching that point. As we move toward our destination, obstacles and distractions emerge. Our clear, unobstructed view of the goal is lost when our eyes focus instead on these situations.

If we hold up our hand and attempt to focus on the background, our hand grows fuzzy and vice versa. Goals and obstacles operate in the same fashion. We cannot focus on both at the same time. It's impossible! As our attention shifts from our dreams to these potential roadblocks, we lose sight of our target. Subsequently we reduce speed so that we might deal with these problems.

However, we possess the ability to handle obstacles without ever losing sight of the goal. In fact, these challenges are easier to tackle if we continue focusing on our target instead. The goal provides motivation and a reason to overcome the obstacle. In other words, we are more determined if we focus just on our dreams! We are more likely to discover a way around these roadblocks. We cannot waste time extinguishing every fire within our line of vision, either. If we are staring at our goal, we can concentrate solely on the blazes that our directly in our path. Conquering only the real challenges is far easier than tackling every potential problem.

Even the best-laid course of action requires adjustments. To prevent straying, keep the goal visible at all times. Like a lion chasing a gazelle, do not lose sight of the prey. Written goals assist greatly in this manner, and visual goals are even more enticing. Keep the target where it can be seen. It does not matter how many times we are required to redirect our path. What counts is reaching and accomplishing our goals.

Goals unite people. Those in a leadership position must ensure that the vision remains clear for everyone involved. When our followers lose sight of the goal, we will need to redirect their path. That may require reminding them of the purpose for this particular course. If the present route is not working or the original path becomes lost, we'll need diplomacy to entice them in the right direction. Remember, suggestion is more effective than force. If followers feel we have their best interests at heart, they will accept our proposals and continue moving toward the goal.

Sometimes distractions cannot be completely avoided. After all, life continues whether we are pursuing a dream or not! A job transfer or a new family member can temporarily derail our forward progress. Deal with these situations as quickly as possible while enjoying the moment as well. When feasible, continue with the quest. It may take a while to get the ball moving again, but eventually we'll find ourselves on track once more.

Critics are the ultimate distraction. Once we set a goal, they appear almost immediately, dogging our every step. We can tune out most of their negative banter by refusing to take the accusations and proclamations personally. Most critics are negative individuals who do not like to see anyone else succeed. Even by ignoring these people, their incessant buzz may still be audible. Like a fly on the window, it is difficult to disregard this annoying sound, especially if they involve others in the process or physically attempt to thwart our progress.

How do we hush critics? We accomplish this task by succeeding! These antagonists are silenced by someone accomplishing what they claim cannot be done. They can't deny the truth at that point. All of their doubt and skepticism is crushed by the simple act of success. When critics attack, simply smile and continue toward the objective. When we reach our goal, we'll discover that most of these people have mysteriously vanished.

Obstacles and distractions can also gain power if the goal is not a burning desire. If we lack passion and excitement, our commitment level will grow weak. Why would we risk encountering challenges for a dream that does not hold our interest? We must believe wholeheartedly in our vision if we ever hope to succeed. This is incredibly vital for leaders. If we want others to follow us, we must be sold on the idea. Select objectives that are truly important and ignite our passion.

"For whatever is true, whatever is worthy of reverence and is honorable and seemly, whatever is just, whatever is pure, whatever is lovely and loveable, whatever is kind and winsome and gracious, if there is any virtue and excellence, if there is anything worthy of praise, think on and weigh and take account of these things- fix your mind on them."
- Bill Wilson, author & Pastor of The Lord's Table

It is this intense desire that will ultimately see us through to victory. Passion will drive our spirit to do whatever it takes to succeed. A cause ignites our soul and no force on earth is more powerful than a person burning with a dream. If we can hold on to that inspiration even when times grow tough, no obstacle will prevent our success. The only real failure is if we fail to try.

What dream resides within you? Are you willing to pursue a goal with passion and purpose? Set a goal and light a fire in your spirit so bright that the entire world will come watch you burn!

In a nutshell...
- We can't focus on goals and obstacles at the same time
- Problems are easier to solve if we remain focused on the goal
- We will need to change course many times
- Motivate followers to stay on target

- Silence critics by succeeding
- Pursue dreams with passion

37

The Five Keys Working Together

Now that we understand the five Keys and their relationship to one another, we can start applying them to our life.

Do not become discouraged if first attempts fall short of the mark. Each Key will take time to master and develop. If it was as simple as flicking a switch, we'd all be leading fulfilled lives right now. The world would be a much happier place if everyone possessed these skills, too! (Regrettably, most believe it easier to remain negative and unfulfilled.) Learning to apply these Keys requires effort, but there are steps we can take to ensure that we continue growing and pursuing the right path.

No matter how monumental or radical the changes in our life, we need to maintain a semblance of balance. A little disruption now and again is fine in the short term, but a life in constant flux will experience only turmoil and frustration. Remember that no one person or thing in this world will make us happy. Balance is essential in all areas or we risk burning out and coming to a screeching halt. It's difficult to pursue dreams if we cannot move.

Remain proactive and in control of all situations. Occasionally exhaustion will cause us to slip back into a negative, reactive state. Catch these momentary lapses before others notice and begin to question. Nothing shakes confidence like an unpredictable leader. Consistency is important, both in our behavior and our thoughts. Become aware of these moments and correct when necessary.

As we grow more confident with the keys, we will experience breakthroughs in achievement. Do not allow this success to cause a false sense of pride. Maintain a humble spirit even in the face of great triumph. Focus on the benefits these victories bring to others instead. This will remind us of what is really important in life. It is when the realization of our dreams touch other's lives that we achieve true success.

Money and stocks notwithstanding, people are the most important assets in the world. Take time to nurture this valuable commodity. (After all, we only get one of us!) Reenergize on all levels, physical and mental. Do not grow so weary that simple tasks are exhausting. The body needs time to heal and we need rest if we are to perform our best. Our minds require moments of peace and quiet reflection to stay sharp. Occasional mindless activities are perfectly acceptable. Do not forget the spirit, either. Stay connected with a source of spiritual inspiration. Take time to recharge all batteries and sharpen the saw.

OVERCOMING

"Busy people only get busier. Get involved in local civic groups and charitable organizations such as the Red Cross, Chamber of Commerce, Habitat For Humanity, and the Arts Council. You will be seen and noticed by the potential customers, clients, and employers while giving back to your community – everybody wins."
- Anne & Johnson Bissette, Bissette Realty

OBSTACLES

Inevitably, a few low points will occur during our journey. Refuse to focus on these bad days or dwell on the negative experiences. Visit the mistake or problem only once and then move along. With every no, every discouragement, we are closer to success.

Avoid the crabs in life. Associate only with positive and successful people and seek to expand this network even further. We can never possess too many friends in high places! Look for individuals that stretch the mind's powers and imagination. These people will inspire our hunger to learn and grow.

Are we still feeding our brain? True leaders never stop learning. Our journey is one of discovery, so continue searching for knowledge and wisdom. Expand the mind with books and the written word. Reading not only provides valuable information, it spurs our imagination to new heights. We learn by writing and planning as well. Take advantage of all opportunities to expand and discover.

"I truly believe reading can help in so many facets of life. The more someone reads, the more they learn. They are exposed to much more through books than through normal everyday life. The more someone reads, the more their vocabulary and reading comprehension will improve. The more a person improves in these areas, the more types of books they are then able to read and enjoy, which builds upon improving these skills."
- Mark Kearney, police officer, literacy consultant, author, and his most important job, a father of two and husband to one, www.bookemfoundation.org

The best method for learning is to teach! This involves all of our senses. When we explain a subject or process in detail, it helps solidify the information in our own minds. Leaders often train their followers, which means good teaching skills are important. In this manner, we pass on the benefits of what we have learned. Consider knowledge a gift!

Return to the five Keys as necessary and keep reaffirming the goal. We need to be reminded of why we are pursuing our chosen path. Keep the dream alive by revisiting it every single day, even if this means posting reminders and prompts in every room of the house! Find a way to keep it planted firmly in the mind and remain emotionally involved and committed.

There are many books on the market today covering aspects of success. Most are based on the same premise, as success principals are universal, but offer different formulas. Within these pages, the five Keys provide a blueprint for success. By focusing on the aspects of a positive attitude, people skills, raising self-esteem, overcoming fear, and setting goals, all of the elements are represented. Whether this system produces results is entirely up to us, though. The success formula that works will be the one we actually apply to our life!

Success is not by chance- it is by choice. Make the decision to apply the five Keys. We can overcome and succeed with a positive attitude, a goal to pursue, and a little SPUNK!

About The Author

Meant to inspire as well as entertain, Wolfe's books have been described as "encouragement personified". She began writing as a teenager and was inspired to return by the adage that everyone needs "something to hope for and someone to love". Ten years associating with a motivation training system and her experience as a foster parent gave her the in-depth knowledge of relationships, personality traits and success principals. The author loves people, and her optimism is fueled by her spunky, sanguine personality.

Wolfe travels extensively promoting her books and has been featured on The Writing Show and CNN Radio. Online she is known as "Spunk On A Stick" and maintains numerous websites and blogs, manages a writer's group, and contributes articles for several other sites. A professional speaker, Wolfe conducts seminars on goal-setting, leadership, publishing & promoting and offers characterization sessions for schools. Her seminar, "Overcoming Obstcles with SPUNK!", is the basis for this book.

A Christian and a foster parent, she facilitates the singles ministry at her church and is involved in numerous literary events & organizations. Wolfe is a professional photographer, a vegetarian, enjoys sports, and has a passion for roller coasters. Originally from Oregon, the author now resides North Carolina with her husband and two cats.

"With a positive attitude, any goal can be achieved!"

www.spunkonastick.net
www.thecircleoffriends.net

Other books by L. Diane Wolfe

THE CIRCLE OF FRIENDS
BOOK I ... LORI
$20.95 ISBN 9780981621005 / 0981621007

To the outside world, Lori Anders has it all. A gifted
swimmer with Olympic dreams, she appears destined
for success. Yet despite her certainty in the pool,
something inhibits Lori from achieving her full potential.
Jason's affections renew her hope and force the shy
swimmer out of her comfort zone. But, will it be
enough to achieve her lifelong dream?

THE CIRCLE OF FRIENDS
BOOK II ... SARAH
$20.95 ISBN 9780981621012 / 0981621015

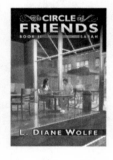

Sarah Martin is bold and intelligent, but she feels
unable to measure up to expectations. When a
friendship suddenly turns romantic, Sarah questions
herself even more. Matt's joyful spirit and social
status appear beyond her reach, yet beneath his
eager smile lies a young man desperate to trust
again. Faced with challenges, they must help each
other come to terms with past disappointments.

THE CIRCLE OF FRIENDS
BOOK III ... JAMES
$19.95 ISBN 9780981621036 / 0981621031

The future appears bright as James Sheppard emerges
from a troubled childhood. However, years of abuse and
loneliness have dampened his spirit. By the time Maria
enters his world, James is nearing the breaking point.
When a crisis abruptly forces him into adulthood, he is
saddled with more responsibility than expected. Will
James find peace before the mistakes of his father
destroy him completely?

THE CIRCLE OF FRIENDS
BOOK IV ... MIKE
$19.95 ISBN 9780981621043 / 098162104X

Mike Taylor is the epitome of stability. Yet beneath the peaceful surface, Mike is consumed with guilt. A former girlfriend's abortion and the intense love he feels for his roommate's wife constantly remind Mike of his failures. Unable to forget and full of shame, he refuses to forgive himself. Will Danielle be able to reach him or is Mike past the point of redemption?

THE CIRCLE OF FRIENDS
BOOK V ... Heather
$19.95 ISBN 9780981621050 / 0981621058

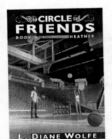

An exciting new beginning coaching Clemson's basketball team awaits Heather Jennings. Unfortunately, her father lies dying of cancer, her sister appears incapable of achievement, and a cocky young player challenges all that remains of her patience. She unexpectedly befriends a smug but appealing young man, but the last thing Heather needs is a serious relationship with a man equally fixated on work and opposed to marriage...

OVERCOMING OBSTACLES WITH SPUNK!
THE KEYS TO LEADERSHIP & GOAL-SETTING
$13.95 ISBN 9780981621029 / 0981621023

Are you ready to break through the barriers obstructing your goals and move into a position of leadership? Then do so with SPUNK! Learn the steps required to overcome obstacles and become an effective leader. The five Keys guide you through developing a positive attitude; learning people skills; raising self-esteem; overcoming fears, and setting goals. Energize your dreams and discover he leader within today!

Above titles may be ordered at your favorite bookstore, retail or online, or order directly from the publisher's website:
www.dancinglemurpress.com

Printed in the United States
145608LV00008BA/124/P